THE BATTLE OF STALINGRAD

THEN AND NOW

THE BATTLE OF STALINGRAD

THEN AND NOW

Edited by Karel Margry

AFTER THE BATTLE

An Imprint of Pen & Sword Books Ltd

The Battle of Stalingrad Then and Now

Published by After the Battle
An imprint of Pen & Sword Books Ltd
47 Church Street, Barnsley,
South Yorkshire, S70 2AS
Tel. 01226 734222
Fax. 01226 734438
Email: enquiries@pen-and-sword.co.uk
Website: **www.afterthebattle.com**
www.pen-and-sword.co.uk

Printed and bound in India by Replika Press Pvt. Ltd.

ISBN: 9781399046268

Commissioning Editor: Rob Green
Editor: Karel Margry
Design: Paul Wilkinson

Credits:
The three chapters of this book were earlier published as articles in *After the Battle* magazine:
'The Battle of Voronezh' by Jason Mark in issue 182 (November 2018);
'Stalingrad' by Mark Holoboski and Alexander Trofimov in issue 166 (November 2014);
'*Stalingrad* – The Film' by Karel Margry in issue 80 (May 1993).

Acknowledgements:
The Editor would like to thank the directorate and staff of the State Panoramic Museum 'Battle of Stalingrad' in Volgograd for helping Alex Trofimov with his research and for making available photos from their archive. For their help with the Battle of Voronezh story, the Editor extends his gratitude to Sergey Popov and Colin Nicol. He also extends his great appreciation to Jason Mark of Leaping Horseman Books for his expert help and for supplying photos from his personal collection. In particular, we acknowledge our debt to Jason's ground-breaking and masterful book *Angriff. The German Attack on Stalingrad in Photos* (Sydney, 2008). The Voronezh chapter is based on his book *Panzerkrieg, Volume 1. German Armoured Operations at Stalingrad. Panzer-Abteilungen 103, 129 and 160* (Sydney, 2017). Mark Holoboski would like to acknowledge the help and support of Vladimir Kalgin, Sergei Petrunin and Russell Schulke over the years.

Photo Credit Abbreviations:
AKG – Archiv für Kultur und Geschichte; ANP – Algemeen Nederlands Persbureau; BA – Bundesarchiv; BA-MA – Bundesarchiv-Militärarchiv; IWM – Imperial War Museum; NIOD – Nederlands Instituut voor Oorlogsdocumentatie, Amsterdam; SZ – Süddeutsche Zeitung Photo; USNA – US National Archives. Unless specified otherwise, all illustrations are from the *After the Battle* archive.

Front Cover: Two NCOs from Panzergrenadier-Regiment 26 of the 24. Panzer-Division taking shelter in a bomb crater on Vokzalnaya Street during the German advance through southern Stalingrad on September 13, 1942 – then and now. An iconic photo of the battle, taken by Kriegsberichter Geller of Panzer-Propaganda-Kompanie 694, it is however a staged picture (see pages 74-75). (NIOD 17283/Alexander Trofimov)

Back Cover:
Top left: German POWs being marched past the Grain Elevator in southern Stalingrad – then and now. (Novosti/Alexander Trofimov)
Top right: Foot soldiers from Infanterie-Regiment 194 of the German 71. Infanterie-Division riding on the deck of a StuG III of Sturmgeschutz-Abteilung 244 on Smolenskaya Street during the German advance into the city on September 16 – then and now. (Novosti/Alexander Trofimov)
Bottom: The German War Cemetery at Rossoshka, 35 kilometres north-west of Volgograd – last burial place of over 60,000 German dead from the Stalingrad battle. (Janelf)

CONTENTS

INTRODUCTION

STALINGRAD WAS NOT ONLY the most-crucial battle on the Eastern Front, it was the main turning point of the whole Second World War in Europe. The Third Reich had suffered setbacks earlier, notably at El Alamein in North Africa in October 1942, but the scale of the fighting on the Eastern Front was incomparably larger than any of the other war fronts and it was the fate of the armies there that decided the outcome of the global conflict. After the demise of the German 6. Armee at Stalingrad in February 1943 it was clear that Nazi Germany would lose the war.

This book brings together three *After the Battle* stories devoted to that historic struggle. It opens with a detailed account of the fight for the city of Voronezh. Lying on the great Don river, it was a prime initial objective of the German summer offensive towards the Caucasus launched on June 28, 1942. Possession of Voronezh would secure an eastern anchor point for a northern defensive line needed for the southward advance to Stalingrad. The city was taken with relative ease in early July but, when the Soviets launched a counter-offensive, the Heeresgruppe Süd commander, Generalfeldmarschall Fedor von Bock, allowed his panzer and motorised divisions to be drawn into the protracted fight. This week-long delay – which infuriated Hitler – severely disrupted the timetable for the main offensive, and fatally contributed to the failure to seize Stalingrad in a surprise raid.

The main part of the book is taken up by a comprehensive description of the gargantuan seven-month battle for Stalingrad itself. All stages are described in detail: the advance of the German armies to the city in August, the stubborn and heroic defence of the besieged Soviet 62nd Army against overwhelming German superiority in September-November; and the subsequent encirclement and annihilation of the doomed 6. Armee in the winter, ending in total capitulation on February 2, 1943.

Due to the wholesale destruction of the embattled city, it was long thought impossible to apply After the Battle's 'then and now' format to Stalingrad but with the help of a local expert and acknowledged student of the battle, Alexander Trofimov, we managed to match up numerous combat photos taken all over the city, giving full treatment to the months-long struggle for the city on the Volga. The same goes for Voronezh where we found another local expert, Sergey Popov, who achieved equally astounding comparisons. Without them, this book could not have been made.

The German catastrophe at Stalingrad, with around 150,000 men killed or succumbing to the winter cold and around 100,000 taken prisoner (of whom only some 5,000 survived captivity), remained a national trauma in Germany. Coming to terms with the event proved difficult, the sorrow over the loss of so many German lives being surmounted by guilt over the fact that Germany had been the aggressor. In many ways, Stalingrad became a taboo, remembered in silence but avoided in public discussion. Illustrative of this is the fact that it took a full 50 years before a major feature film on Stalingrad could be produced in Germany. It was only in 1992 that the German film industry felt the time was ripe and produced and released *Stalingrad*, the first full-fledged war movie on the battle. We include the story of the making of this film as an epilogue to the main story.

Karel Margry, *Editor*

German soldiers being marched off into captivity on the Square of Fallen Heroes in the centre of Stalingrad after the surrender of the German 6. Armee on February 2, 1943. (Novosti)

THE BATTLE OF VORONEZH

By Jason Mark

THE FAILURE OF OPERATION 'BARBAROSSA' to knock the Soviet Union out of the war in 1941 almost brought the Wehrmacht to its knees when the Red Army struck back during the frigid winter of 1941-42 with a series of successful counter-offensives. Despite this almost fatal setback, Hitler still desired an offensive solution, so as winter drew to an end, the Oberkommando des Heeres (OKH – German Army High Command) began to develop plans for a 1942 offensive. Germany's insufficient oil reserves and inability to conduct a prolonged war determined the objective: the Caucasian

In early July 1942, the German armies on the Eastern front, as part of Heeresgruppe Süd's renewed summer offensive and southward drive towards the Caucasus (Operation 'Blau'), attacked and captured the strategic city of Voronezh. Lying just east of the great Don river, the city was taken in a concentric attack by four divisions – one armoured and three motorised – striking out from two newly captured bridgeheads. The Russian defenders were no match for the Germans and, despite Stalin sending in reinforcements from his strategic reserve and ordering counter-attacks to retake the city, the Soviets lost heavily, especially in men and tanks. However, the protracted fight for the city kept the German armour engaged in the Voronezh area longer than expected, upsetting the timetable for the main offensive and fatally delaying the operation to capture Stalingrad. This picture of tanks of Panzer-Abteilung 103, part of the motorised 3. Infanterie-Division, in the northern part of the city was taken on July 7. (BA Bild 101I-216-0436-07A)

oilfields. Fortunately for the Ostheer (German Army on the Eastern front), the spring thaw, general exhaustion and overextended supply lines halted Soviet operations and allowed it to catch its breath and to rebuild. Warmer weather resurrected German spirits and slowly dissipated the taint of winter defeats. A resounding triumph over a Soviet counter-offensive at Kharkov in May 1942 signified that the Ostheer was once again in fine mettle.

The German summer offensive, code-named 'Fall Blau', consisted of a three-pronged attack by Generalfeldmarschall Fedor von Bock's Heeresgruppe Süd that aimed to destroy Red Army forces in the south and capture the oilfields. Generaloberst Hermann Hoth's 4. Panzer-Armee and Generaloberst Maximilian von Weichs's 2. Armee, supported by Colonel-General Gusztav Jany's Hungarian Second Army, would attack from Kursk to Voronezh and then continue south-east along the Don river to anchor the northern flank of the offensive on the Volga river. General der Panzertruppe Friedrich Paulus's 6. Armee would advance from Kharkov parallel with Hoth's army to the Volga, while Generaloberst Ewald von Kleist's 1. Panzer-Armee plunged south towards the lower Don with the 17. Armee on its western flank and the Rumanian Fourth Army to its east.

The initial objective for Hoth's 4. Panzer-Armee was the strategically important city of Voronezh. In the summer of 1942, Voronezh – a major provincial city of 326,840 people and the administrative centre of Voronezh Oblast – was less than 200 kilometres from the front line. Straddling the Voronezh river, a tributary of the Don, the city was a vital transportation hub between Moscow – over 500 kilometres to the north – and southern Russia,

Our comparison photographs for this story were taken by Sergey Popov, a resident of the city and long-time student of the 1942 battle. This is the same spot at the junction of Donbasskaya Street and Plekhanovskaya Street, near Voronezh Railway Station II, today. The multi-storey apartment block on the right still stands (see also page 29-30).
(Sergey Popov)

with railways and arterial roads radiating in all four directions. Industrial areas in its northern and western districts contained mills, bakeries and enterprises that processed cattle products (meat, tallow, soap and hides). When the Wehrmacht crossed the border on June 22, 1941, many of the city's manufacturing facilities converted to military production: the excavator factory helped develop the Katyusha rocket-launcher, while other complexes turned out radios, diesel motors, aircraft engines, locomotives and rolling stock. On the city's outskirts were two airfields.

Armeegruppe Weichs (the northern grouping of Heeresgruppe Süd) formed the northern pincer of a double envelopment that aimed to surround the Soviet 40th and 21st Armies and then exploit to the Don river. On its northern wing was Weichs's own 2. Armee with three infantry corps; in the middle was Hoth's 4. Panzer-Armee with – from north to south – General der Infanterie Erich Straube's XIII. Armee-Korps, General der Panzertruppe Willibald Freiherr von Langermann's XXIV. Panzer-Korps and General der Panzertruppe Werner Kempf's XXXXVIII. Panzer-Korps, and protecting the southern flank was Jany's Hungarian Second Army with two infantry corps.

Opposing Weichs were Lieutenant-General Mikhail Parsegov's 40th Army with six rifle divisions and three rifle brigades, Major-General Aleksei Danilov's 21st Army with nine rifle divisions and two rifle brigades, and elements of Major-General Nikolai Pukhov's 13th Army.

Kempf's XXXXVIII. Panzer-Korps, fielding 280 panzers, comprised Generalmajor Bruno Ritter von Hauenschild's 24. Panzer-Division, Generalmajor Sigfrid Henrici's 16. Infanterie-Division (mot.) and Generalmajor Walter Hörnlein's Grossdeutschland-Division (mot.), all high-quality formations. Langermann's XXIV. Panzer-Korps, comprising the 9. Panzer-Division, 3. Infanterie-Division (mot.) and 377. Infanterie-Division (and reinforced with the 11. Panzer-Division on July 4), had 353 panzers.

The Red Army held a slight numerical superiority in armour: Parsegov's 40th Army possessed roughly 70 tanks in two brigades, while the 16th Tank Corps with 180 tanks was in the army's rear; Danilov's 21st Army was supported by the 13th Tank Corps (163 tanks) and could also call upon the 4th Tank Corps (145 tanks) and 24th Tank Corps (141 tanks) – giving a total of 699 tanks compared to 633 on the German side.

THE START OF THE OFFENSIVE

Armeegruppe Weichs initiated 'Blau' at dawn on June 28 with a 30-minute artillery barrage and air strikes. Mechanised infantry breached the Soviet defences and the armour slipped through. The terrain was almost perfect tank country: gently rolling grasslands with occasional patches of woodland, the only obstacle being the many waterways. Oberst Gustav-Adolf Riebel's Panzer-Regiment 24 of the 24. Panzer-Division seized an intact railway bridge over the Tim river – lit fuses and explosive charges were ripped off in the nick of time – and then rolled on to the Kshen river. Other divisions achieved similar

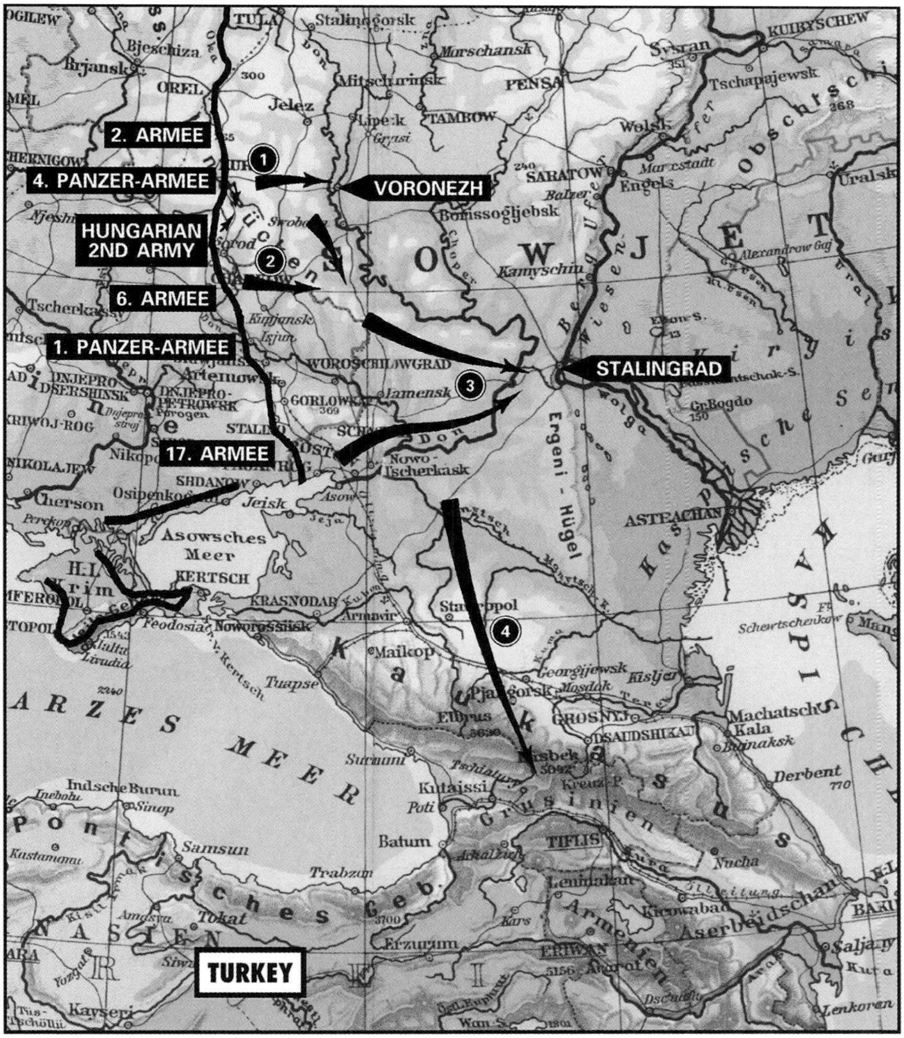

Operation 'Blau' was to comprise four phases. Voronezh was to be captured in Phase 1 after which the 4. Panzer-Armee and 6. Armee were to join in a southward advance towards Stalingrad, followed by a push into the Caucasus.

progress, yet an ill-timed downpour in the evening threatened to scuttle the entire operation, the sodden ground immobilising some units for days.

Kempf's mobile formations continued to churn eastward on June 29. After crossing the Kshen and covering almost 30 kilometres with the Grossdeutschland echeloned to its left, the 24. Panzer-Division overran 40th Army headquarters in Bykovo and just missed capturing General Parsegov and his staff. Stukas mistakenly bombed the spearheads of both divisions, even though aerial recognition panels were displayed, because the pilots believed that no German unit could have penetrated so far. As night fell, the campaign's first major tank duel erupted near the villages of Bykovo and Gorshechnoye and continued into June 30. Oberst Riebel's panzers bloodied their opponents, claiming 28 tanks, mostly KVs and T-34s, though not without loss. During the engagement, Leutnant Herbert Cornelius, a platoon leader in the 5. Schwadron of Panzer-Regiment 24, narrowly escaped death:

'While I was informing my gunner about a tank I had spotted, I saw its muzzle flash. Firing at the same time as us, its shell struck our gun mantlet and with a loud crack shoved the whole cannon deep into the turret, causing me to hit the back of my head against the turret wall and lose consciousness.'

Although the southern wing of the 40th Army held the Hungarians west of the Tim, Soviet leaders realised that unless Weichs was stopped, his panzers would gain operational freedom, fan out and trap most of the 40th Army. The situation deteriorated further for the Soviets on June 30 when Paulus's 6. Armee set off and quickly coalesced into a second pincer that threatened the entire Southwestern Front of Marshal of the Soviet Union Semyon Timoshenko. The breakneck pace was maintained over the following days. By July 2, the 24. Panzer-Division had cracked enemy resistance around Stary Oskol and opened the way to the Don river and Voronezh.

In response to the German attack, Lieutenant-General Filipp Golikov's Bryansk Front was renamed the Voronezh Front. On July 2, after incurring disastrous losses, the Stavka (Soviet Armed Forces High Command) released Lieutenant-General Maksim Antoniuk's 3rd Reserve Army to take up positions north of Voronezh. Once in situ, it was renamed 60th Army. At this point, Stalin still believed the German offensive was a prelude to an advance on Moscow.

On July 4, Langermann pivoted his 9. and 11. Panzer-Divisions north-eastward to form a cordon, together with the infantry divisions of the XIII. Armee-Korps, to protect the northern flank of the main axis of advance to Voronezh. At the same time, the spearheads of Kempf's XXXXVIII. Panzer-Korps – the Grossdeutschland and the 24. Panzer-Division, followed by the 16. Infanterie-Division (mot.) – rushed towards the Don river. The only forces defending Voronezh were weak NKVD security forces, air defence units, rear service elements of the 40th Army and the immobile 75th and 53rd Fortified Regions.

BRIDGEHEADS ACROSS THE DON

The Grossdeutschland and the 24. Panzer-Division agreed to establish as many bridgeheads over the Don as possible for a concentric attack on Voronezh.

On July 4, Kampfgruppe Hellermann from the 24. Panzer-Division, under Oberstleutnant Vollrath von Hellermann, commander of Kradschützen-Abteilung 4, seized Siniye-Lipyagi and established a bridgehead over the Don at Rudkino, 35 kilometres south-south-west of Voronezh.

Further north, Oberst Maximilian von Edelsheim's Schützen-Regiment 26 and two-thirds of Oberst Riebel's Panzer-Regiment 24 captured an intact but rickety bridge over the Don at Yunevka. The latter village lay just north of the confluence of the Don and its tributary, the Voronezh river, and some 18 kilometres closer to Voronezh city than Rudkino. From there one could

Operation 'Blau' and the race to the Don began on June 28. Seven days into the offensive, on July 4, Kampfgruppe Hellermann of the 24. Panzer-Division captured a ferry landing at Rudkino and established a bridgehead, thus becoming the first German troops to reach and cross the upper Don. Further north, Schützen-Regiment 26 captured a bridge over the Don near Yunevka/Malyshevo, but it was in such poor condition that only foot soldiers could cross. Engineers worked all through the night of July 4/5 to repair and strengthen the span's sagging central support, and tanks of Panzer-Regiment 24 began crossing in the morning. This is Rittmeister Ulrich von Mirbach's 1. Schwadron of the I. Abteilung traversing the river. Sitting in the cupola of '131' is Leutnant Cay-Lorenz Baron von Brockdorff, leader of the squadron's 3. Zug (and future Knight's Cross winner). All three battalions of the regiment were across before noon. (NAC)

A single-lane pontoon bridge, installed in the 1970s, now connects the riverbanks. Malyshevo is still very rural, but its eastern neighbour, Shilovo, boasts large apartment complexes that arose concurrently with the construction of a nuclear power plant that began in 1983. (Voronezh residents voted overwhelmingly in 1990 to halt its construction). (Sergey Popov)

advance directly to the city, the main part of which lay on the west bank of the Voronezh, whereas from Rudkino one could only make an approach along the east bank of the Voronezh towards the suburbs on the east bank. It was obvious that an attack towards the city could better be launched from the Yunevka bridgehead. An advance from the Rudkino bridgehead to attack Voronezh from the east was stymied by strong resistance and was consequently abandoned.

In the Grossdeutschland sector, Oberleutnant Carl Ludwig Blumenthal, leading the 7. Kompanie of Oberst Otto Köhler's Infanterie-Regiment 'Grossdeutschland' 1, seized the village of Semiluki, 12 kilometres west of Voronezh, late on July 4 and charged its Don road bridge with one of its

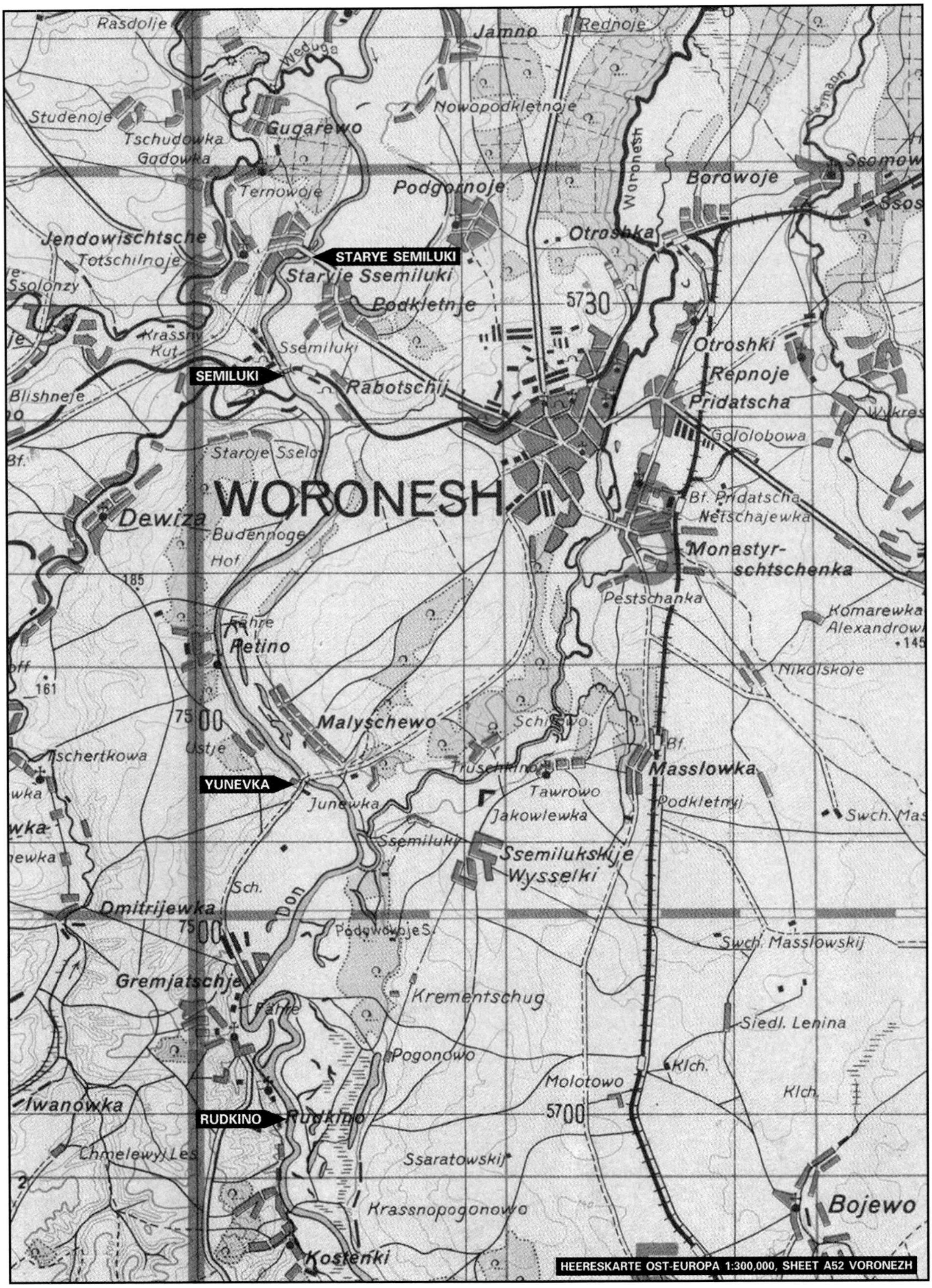

While the 24. Panzer-Division established bridgeheads over the Don at Rudkino and Yunevka, the Grossdeutschland Division did the same further north, at Starye Semiluki and Semiluki. This enabled the two divisions to launch a concentric attack on the city from the south-west and west. The Yunevka bridgehead was then later used by the 16. Infanterie-Division and the one at Starye Semiluki by the 3. Infanterie-Division when these formations were ordered to take over the battle. (Jason Mark)

By mid-morning on July 6, the 24. Panzer-Division had captured the southern outskirts of Voronezh and the undamaged southern bridge over the Voronezh river, thus sealing off an important retreat route for Soviet troops. The following morning (July 7), a strong combat group – comprising Schützen-Regiment 21 and the armoured squadrons of Kradschützen-Abteilung 4 and Schützen-Regiment 26 – was assembled at the southern end of Ulitsa 20-letiya Oktyabrya (20th Anniversary of October Street), a few hundred metres uphill from the bridge embankment, in preparation for a push into the city. An official photographer, Kriegsberichter Klaus Niermann of Luftwaffe-Kriegsberichter-Kompanie 8, joined the force. One of his first shots showed an SdKfz 251 half-track of the I. Abteilung of Schützen-Regiment 26 moving up Baltiyskiy Alley, a minor road branching off 20-letiya Oktyabrya (see the town plan on page 19). (BA Bild 101I-452-0997-10A)

Still a nondescript back alley today. (Sergey Popov)

platoons. Despite fire from bunkers on the opposite bank, Blumenthal and a few men sprinted across, established a toe-hold and doused small fires on the wooden structure while Unteroffizier Hempel, neck-deep in the water, tore off explosives and burning fuses with his bare hands. Blumenthal pulled back his small garrison under the cover of darkness. Although fire destroyed a 15-metre section of the bridge, Blumenthal and his men captured the eastern approaches the following morning, July 5.

Four kilometres further south, near the Semiluki railway bridge, the I. Bataillon (Hauptmann Theodor Bethke) and III. Bataillon (Hauptmann

Assault groups formed by armoured personnel carriers and panzers swept north along individual streets, flushing out and eliminating Soviet defenders. This T-60 light tank was caught at the crossroads of 20-letiya Oktyabrya Street and Novo Slobodskaya/Kirova Streets. It almost certainly belonged to the 181st Tank Brigade – holding position in the area of the meat-packing plant on Koltsovskaya Street – which at 8 a.m. that morning had despatched a four-tank platoon into the city on reconnaissance. 'All were destroyed', noted the brigade's combat journal.

The apartment building still stands today, though with the addition of a new wing. (Sergey Popov)

Prüss) of Oberst Eugen Garski's Infanterie-Regiment 'Grossdeutschland' 2 paddled across the Don in inflatable rafts once darkness fell on July 5. The crossing took most of the night and as dawn broke on July 6, both battalions had assembled on the east bank, ready to attack eastward to Podkletnoye station. Good initial headway was stalled first by determined resistance from the station buildings, then minefields on a line of hills, and finally by flanking fire from the village of Podkletnoye, a kilometre to the north. No progress could be made until this village was taken by Köhler's Infanterie-Regiment 'Grossdeutschland' 1.

Assault guns were the first vehicles to cross Blumenthal's repaired bridge and joined the infantry outside Podkletnoye at around 0900 hours. Difficult combat in blazing heat sapped the infantrymen's strength, but they eventually cleared Soviet troops from the nearby woods and troop training grounds. Following the capture of Podkletnoye, two companies of the I. Bataillon of

Infanterie-Regiment 'Grossdeutschland' 1 clambered aboard the assault guns and sortied towards Voronezh, pushing deep into the city and reaching Voronezh II Railway Station, the freight and marshalling yards. Though soon called back, they laid claim to being the first German troops in the city.

Hoth was under strict instructions not to let his mobile formations become ensnared in urban combat as they were needed for the second phase of the offensive, yet as it appeared the Soviets were abandoning the city, Heeresgruppe Süd allowed motorised troops to occupy it. Four such divisions were converging on Voronezh, but the two actually in position to take the city – the Grossdeutschland and the 24. Panzer-Division – had been ordered to pull back and head south. The task of taking Voronezh thus fell to the 3. and 16. Infanterie-Divisions (mot.). This all happened at the moment Stalin ordered the Red Army to hold the city or recapture it.

PENETRATION OF THE CITY

At 0800 hours on July 5, the three battalions of Oberst Riebel's Panzer-Regiment 24 drove single file over the Don bridge at Yunevka, repaired overnight by divisional engineers. Major Dietrich von der Lancken, commander of the regiment's III. Abteilung, recorded events in a private log:

The trams are gone, the rails removed, and the Voronezh Circus now fills the park. (Sergey Popov)

Panzer '214' of Panzer-Regiment 24 rolls north past Tram No. 56 on 20-letiya Oktyabrya, just south of the Y-junction with Koltsovskaya. Note the aerial recognition flag draped across the front, a sensible precaution considering the number of Stukas in the air. Behind the tram is the Park of Culture and Rest, known locally as the 'Park of the Living and the Dead' because it was a converted cemetery that had been in use until 1935 (marked [C] on the town plan on page 19). (NIOD 60320)

Oberleutnant Klaus Nordmann, adjutant of the I. Abteilung of Panzer-Regiment 24, flattens a sapling in Panzer III '362' while taking a short-cut across a park on the north-western corner of the Y-junction. Twenty-four hours later, the street in the distance would be a scene of carnage (see pages 34-39). Kriegsberichter Niermann used two cameras, one with regular black-and-white film, the other with rare colour stock.

A hamburger restaurant and a pharmacy now fill the space. (Sergey Popov)

'In a small patch of woods two kilometres north-east of the bridge, the attack was readied. The regiment moved off at 1400 hours north-east towards Voronezh. To our left, separated by an enemy-occupied forest, was the II. Abteilung, while echeloned steeply backwards on the right was the I. Abteilung. Against slight infantry resistance, a hill three kilometres south-west of the outskirts, which offered an excellent view of the city, was occupied. Suddenly, ten T-34s appeared in front of the battalion. In a fierce engagement, eight enemy tanks are destroyed. A further advance into the city encountered strong resistance. Anti-tank guns, anti-aircraft guns and even dug-in tanks secured the edge of the city. In accordance with orders, the battalion hedge-hogged for the night on the high ground.'

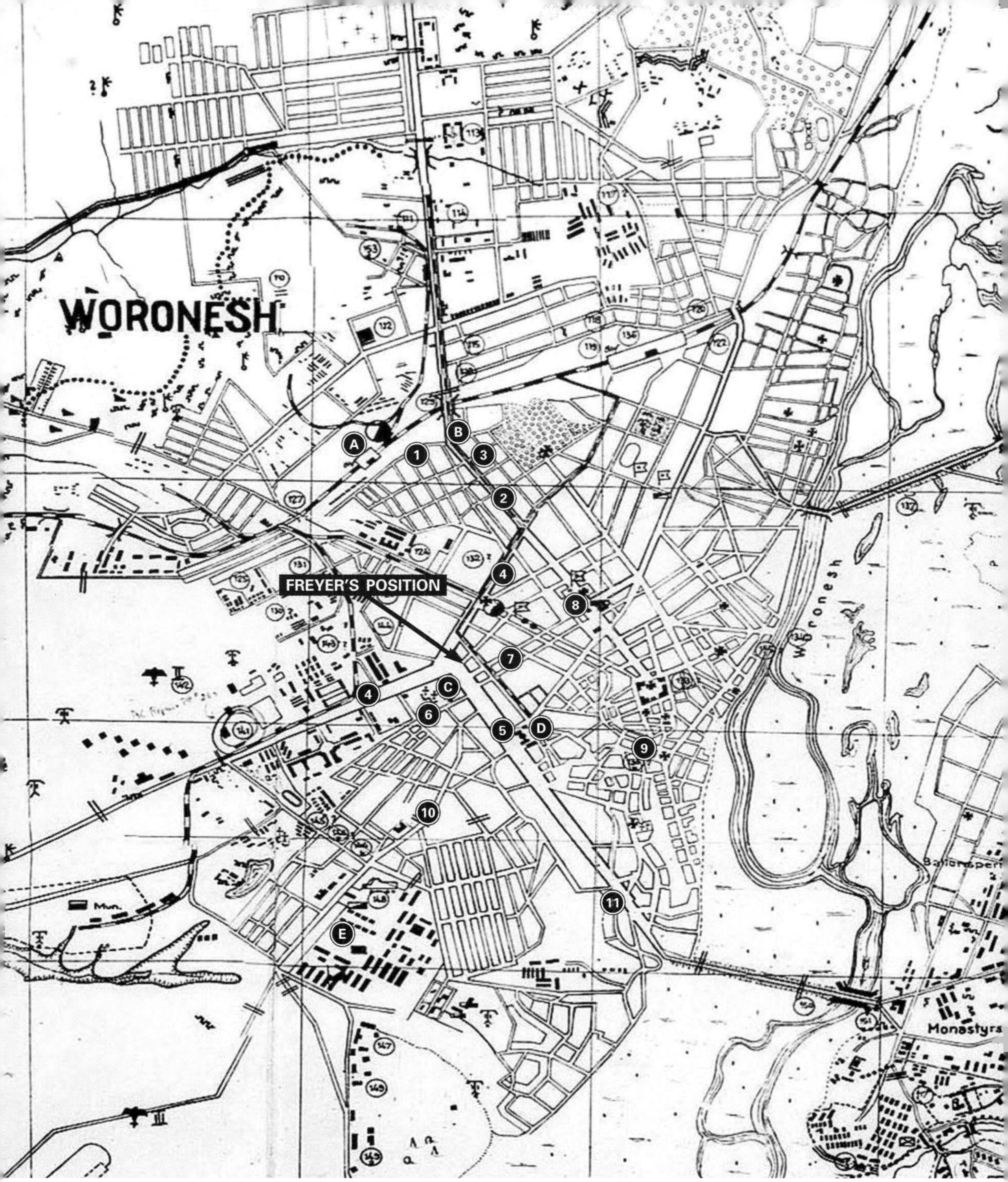

This town plan of Voronezh was produced by Vermessungs- und Karten-Abteilung 620 (a 4. Panzer-Armee mapping unit) on July 3, 1942 from a captured Red Army map, German Air Ministry intelligence and aerial photos. We have indicated the streets and locations that feature in our story. [1] Plekhanovskaya Street. [2] Donbasskaya Street. [3] 3rd Internatsionala Street. [4] Koltsovskaya Street (western part today named Voroshilova Street). [5] 20-letiya Oktyabrya Street. [6] Novo Slobodskaya Street (today Moiseyeva Street). [7] Kirova Street. [8] 20th Anniversary of October Square (today Lenin Square). [9] Bolshaya Streletskaya Street. [10] Krasnoznamonnaya Street. [11] Baltiyskiy Alley. [A] Voronezh Railway Station II. [B] Voroshilovskaya Polyclinic. [C] Park of Culture and Rest. [D] Voronezh Aviation Institute. [E] Chizhov Military Barracks. (Jason Mark)

Single panzers positioned themselves at key junctions to secure the location against enemy tanks. Niermann pictured Panzer '224' sitting at the intersection of Koltsovskaya and Plekhanovskaya Streets. As shown in the preceding frames of his film, one half-track squadron of the I. Abteilung of Schützen-Regiment 26 had already rolled past en route to the city's main square. (BA Bild 101I-452-0997-31A)

Voronezh has seen extensive development since the war and the quiet intersection of 1942 is today a busy juncture overlooked by multi-storey blocks. (Sergey Popov)

The following day (July 6), Major Josef Fau's Kradschützen-Bataillon 53 of Generalmajor Helmuth Schlömer's 3. Infanterie-Division (mot.) gained a foothold over the Don north of Semiluki village and erected a strong northward-facing flank across to Podkletnoye. That night, General Schlömer received the order to relieve the Grossdeutschland.

Insertion of Oberst Walter Denkert's Infanterie-Regiment 8 (mot.) into its allocated sector on July 7 was delayed by the Grossdeutschland columns moving in the opposite direction across the only bridge. Major Hans-Joachim Schepers's Sturmgeschütz-Abteilung 'Grossdeutschland' was left behind for 24 hours to support Schlömer's division. Piggybacking a company from Oberst August-Wilhelm Küster's Infanterie-Regiment 29 (mot.), its 3. Batterie pushed into Voronezh in an attempt to become the first German unit to take the city, but was recalled.

A combat report prepared by Oberst Wilhelm Lengerke's Schützen-Regiment 21 of the 24. Panzer-Division reveals that division's methodical assault into the metropolis from the south:

> 'As July 7 dawned, the armoured squadrons of Kradschützen-Abteilung 4 and Schützen-Regiment 26 were placed under the control of our combat group. Using the armoured half-tracks, other shock troops were set up to establish and maintain contact with the strongpoints

Niermann's next shot shows what the commander of '224' was looking out for: a column of motorcycle sidecars and half-tracks from the same battalion, each vehicle travelling 50 metres apart, rolling north-eastwards along Koltsovskaya. Resembling a victory parade rather than an incursion into the depths of an enemy metropolis, the single-column deployment shows that the Germans anticipated little resistance. (BA Bild 101I-452-0997-32A)

Six lanes of traffic now fill Koltsovskaya Street. Buildings like these, typical of 1930s Soviet architecture, are colloquially known as 'Stalinkas ('Stalin's Houses'). The former government building today houses banks, a post office and retail stores. (Sergey Popov)

and should also drive along individual streets to clear them, exactly according to plan. Single tanks were deployed at key intersections to shoot up enemy tanks.

'The operation, prepared down to the smallest detail, succeeded. By midday, after the elimination of local resistance, the southern part of the city was firmly in our hands. Although only Panzer-Schwadron Spannocchi [led by Rittmeister Emil Spannocchi] could be deployed, since the rest were halted due to fuel shortages, riflemen and panzer crews with assigned pioneers held all points reached. Reconnaissance pushed out to the railway determined that other German troops were nowhere in the city. On the other hand, the pressure of our troops attacking from the west and north-west was noticeable around midday. Before this attack, the Russians pressed against the city centre to reach the only intact southern bridge and gain the eastern bank. Numerous tanks, mostly T-34s, appeared, either individually or in groups.'

As part of the 24. Panzer-Division attack from the south, a half-track platoon from the 2. Schwadron of Kradschützen-Abteilung 4, escorted by some

By midday, with the southern half of Voronezh apparently in German hands, Niermann returned to the starting point of the day's operation at the southern end of 20-letiya Oktyabrya Street. On the right, Oberst Fritz von Broich, commander of Schützen-Brigade 24 (wearing the German Cross in Gold on his breast pocket), is briefed on the situation by his battalion commanders. In the middle, awaiting orders, is Leutnant Hubertus Schulz, commander of the 2. Zug of the 2. Schwadron of Kradschützen-Abteilung 4 (wearing a peaked officer's cap). The SdKfz 250/3 command half-track belongs to the I. Bataillon of Schützen-Regiment 26. Visible in the distance, on the far side of the Voronezh river, is the city power station. (BA Bild 101I-452-0997-36A)

The house on the right has gone but vehicles still park on the open area today. Construction of the Voronezh Reservoir in the early 1970s widened and raised the river, making it far more visible today than in 1942. (Sergey Popov)

panzers, reconnoitred into the southern part of the city. Patrol leader was Leutnant Hubertus Schulz:

> 'We drove north into the city on a wide arterial road, the vehicles at 50-metre intervals. Watching carefully in all directions, we groped our way from intersection to intersection. Nothing moved. Suddenly, an avenue tree about 100 metres ahead of us seemed to be moving. I stopped and watched through the binoculars. I distinctly recognised two well-camouflaged T-34s, which turned their barrels on us and opened fire a little later. We threw smoke-candles and I ordered "Dismount and vehicles back!" We jumped out of the vehicles and dispersed into the houses alongside the road. Due to the distance between vehicles, the platoon split apart and every man was on his own.
>
> 'The enemy tanks advanced and one secured directly to our right. We tried to attach a hollow-charge mine, but the tank kept moving before we could arm the detonator. Suddenly the street came alive. Shots whipped from all directions. We sought protection in the partially burned-out houses.
>
> 'After a while, the tanks returned at high speed; they had been taken under fire by our anti-tank guns, set up in a cross-street. That

Shortly after midday, Leutnant Schulz was ordered to lead a combat reconnaissance into the city and link up with a patrol from the Grossdeutschland Division at the railway station. His Kampfgruppe consisted of his own platoon of eight half-tracks (one armed with a 3.7cm PaK anti-tank gun, the others with machine guns), a few other half-tracks from the 1. and 3. Schwadrons, plus tanks from the 2. Schwadron of Panzer-Regiment 24. Here, the group pauses half-way along 20-letiya Oktyabrya, opposite the Voronezh Aviation Institute. Although the street had been swept a few hours earlier, Schulz still proceeded with caution due to reports of Soviet tanks roving the area. (Jason Mark)

The building on the right had been the Voronezh Engineering and Construction Institute until mid-June 1941, when it became the Voronezh Aviation Institute. Today it is the Voronezh State University of Architecture and Civil Engineering. (Sergey Popov)

After battling two T-34s, Schulz's patrol halted on Plekhanovskaya Street just before the intersection with 3rd Internatsionala Street, barely two blocks from the railway station. On the right is Panzer '224', seen earlier guarding the intersection at the southern end of Plekhanovskaya. Smoke billows from a fuel storage depot north of the railway line. Schulz and his men – including Oberwachtmeister Willy Neubacher, commander of the 3. Zug – left their vehicles and advanced towards the station on foot to meet the Grossdeutschland patrol, but nobody was there. Schulz subsequently pulled back his patrol. (Jason Mark)

A large building (just off the picture on the right) prevented Sergey from taking a more-accurate comparison but the large residential complex remains though since modified by the addition of two new wings that now enclose its U-shaped courtyard. (Sergey Popov)

was the end of the scare. Even small-arms fire stopped once their tank protection had disappeared.

'The platoon rallied and we proceeded on foot to the station, only encountering individual resistance nests. Since we could not find Grossdeutschland troops far and wide, we retired to our vehicles and started our return trip. This reconnaissance revealed that the city was still occupied by infantry forces that were more or less fighting in isolated groups.'

With no apparent cohesive defence, Rittmeister Ulrich von Mirbach, commander of the 1. Schwadron of Panzer-Regiment 24, was ordered to block the northern road bridge over the Voronezh river with his squadron and an attached company of panzer grenadiers:

'The grenadiers sat on the back of the panzers and safeguarded them against close-combatants, but we saw neither enemy soldiers nor civilians in our advance to the northern outskirts. The city seemed

The Grossdeutschland Division – the northern prong of the concentric attack on Voronezh – had crossed the Don river at two places near Semiluki on July 4 and from these bridgeheads had conducted two forays into the city. The first, on July 6, had reached Voronezh Railway Station II, but the second on July 7 was recalled because orders had been received to hand over operations to the 3. Infanterie-Division. This explains why Leutnant Schulz did not find any Grossdeutschland troops at the station. The division pulled out of the battle, withdrawing back over the Don and moving south to re-join Heeresgruppe Süd's main offensive. Here assault guns from Sturmgeschütz-Abteilung 'Grossdeutschland' head south along the west bank of the Veduga river, a small stream running four kilometres west of the Don, near the village of Yendovishche.

Having held the northern flank of the XXXXVIII. Panzer-Korps front for two days, the 3. Infanterie-Division was ordered to take over the Grossdeutschland Division's sector north of Voronezh late on July 6. This shot, by Kriegsberichter Koch of Propaganda-Kompanie 694, shows the relief underway. Panzer IIs from the 3. Kompanie of Panzer-Abteilung 103 (the tank battalion attached to the 3. Infanterie-division) cross the Veduga river near Yendovishche en route for Voronezh, while Grossdeutschland infantrymen move in the opposite direction. (BA Bild 101I-216-0435-29)

The Church of the Intercession seen on the bluff in the background was Sergey's key to identifying the location of these two pictures. Having stood for over two centuries, it was almost completely destroyed during the war. Today, a new church is being built in a different style a hundred metres or so from the original site. With trees and undergrowth along the riverbank blocking the view, this is the best comparison possible. (Sergey Popov)

to be completely deserted. Driving to the north-east, based on the position of the smoke-tinted sun, we reached the riverside road just short of the north bridge after just half an hour. We halt and observe if the riverbank is enemy-occupied. Leutnant [Cay-Lorenz Baron] von Brockdorf drove up alongside my panzer at the front and requested permission to take the bridge with his platoon. My answer: No, but put enemy bridge guards under fire! After the first bursts of fire, the Russians blew up the bridge! We were about 150 metres away and saw the piles of the wooden bridge whirl through the air like matchsticks.'

Other panzers and half-tracks also pressed into the eerily deserted city. A report by Panzer-Regiment 24 perfectly captures the atmosphere:

> 'Metre by metre, the fighting eats its way into the city. The heat of the large burning apartment blocks, together with gun fumes, lies over the thoroughfares. The bright façades stand out from the black clouds of smoke from the huge fires caused by our bombing attacks.'

Rittmeister Rudolf von Knebel-Doberitz, commander of the 3. Schwadron of Schützen-Regiment 21, inadvertently stumbled into a tank nest:

> 'In the morning, after a nocturnal operation, my squadron was designated regimental reserve and sent to "get some sleep" in a large barracks block about two kilometres behind the regimental command post. Fortunately, the squadron marched there in battle formation and with reconnaissance out in front because the barracks proved to be enemy-occupied, namely by tanks.
>
> 'The squadron settled down on the upper floors of several barracks buildings, but was then virtually encircled by the enemy tanks, which surrounded the buildings and kept them under fire. In the afternoon, with the support of the 9. Schwadron of Panzer-Regiment 24 as well as the attack by our 6. and 7. Schwadrons, the barracks complex was mopped up, from which 36 enemy tanks broke out towards the city centre. We were able to report this break-out by radio in time, and our panzers managed to knock out all of those tanks.'

On the opposite (northern) side of town, the 3. Infanterie-Division continued to thicken its defensive line across the interfluve between the Don and Voronezh rivers. Oberst Küster's Infanterie-Regiment 29 formed the mainstay, but it was backed by 88mm guns, artillery assets and two panzer companies held in reserve in tattered aircraft hangars. Major Fau's motorcycle battalion scooted north to overlook the Zadonsk highway and control the adjacent woodlands. On the western outskirts, two battalions of Denkert's Infanterie-Regiment 8 attacked along the main road into Voronezh at 1600 hours: the I. Bataillon (Major Blume) advanced north of the road and the II. Bataillon (Major Scholze) south of it, while Oberleutnant Werner Kunz's 2. Kompanie of Panzer-Abteilung 103 (Major Jobst von Reinhardt) stuck close to the roadway because the panzers required its bridge to traverse a gully and

With Grossdeutschland units pulling back westward across the Semiluki bridge, the 3. Infanterie-Division required its own crossing over the Don. A Soviet engineers' bridge at Starye Semiluki, north of Semiluki, had been seized mostly intact. The Germans replaced the missing eastern half with pontoons and metal bridging sections and Panzer-Abteilung 103 began crossing on July 7, as seen in this picture by Koch. The tanks maintained strict spacing in order to spread the loading on the bridge and the heaviest vehicles, the Panzer IVs, crossed the span individually, maximum speed being set at eight kilometres per hour. On the horizon, providing cover for the crossing point, is an SdKfz 10/4 self-propelled 2cm anti-aircraft gun. (BA Bild 101-216-0435-39)

The crossing site remains unchanged, though nowadays the vegetation is considerably lusher. In 1942 there was a blown road bridge just a few hundred metres upstream from here but today it has been replaced by a modern highway bridge. (Sergey Popov)

The missed rendezvous with Schulz's patrol prompted the 3. Infanterie-Division to despatch its own combat patrol to the station late on July 7. The force consisted of the tanks of Oberleutnant Werner Kunz's 2. Kompanie of Panzer-Abteilung 103, with the men of Oberleutnant Bernhard Sittig's 7. Kompanie of Infanterie-Regiment 8 riding on the decks. Two war photographers, Koch and Sautter, the latter also from Propaganda-Kompanie 694, accompanied the force. Squatting behind the turret of one of the tanks, Sautter pictured the column as it trundled into the city via Donbasskaya Street. On the right are outbuildings of Voronezh Railway Station II. (BA Bild 101I-216-0431-25)

Travelling on another vehicle, Koch pictured Panzer '241', the mount of Hauptfeldwebel Hans Walz, platoon leader of the 4. Zug (and a future Knight's Cross holder), ploughing through the pall of a smouldering T-60. (BA Bild 101I-216-0436-05)

tank ditch. Against strengthening resistance, the city fringe was reached at 1945 hours, but it was impossible for every house to be properly searched. The infantrymen had only penetrated 500 metres into the built-up zone by twilight. Oberleutnant Kunz wanted to slice through to the Voronezh river with his panzers and convinced Oberleutnant Bernhard Sittig, commander of the 7. Kompanie of Infanterie-Regiment 8, to come along:

> 'Two panzers, without troops mounted, would be up front, all others would have infantry on them. Oberleutnant Kunz drove the third panzer and I sat next to him on the turret. We should really have travelled on different panzers but this made communication easier. All available panzers were quickly occupied and covered with riflemen. The pair up front, however, remained devoid of soldiers. We took off. The first panzer only boomed a few times along the streets in the approaching darkness, and everything quickly became quiet. We moved very slowly through the city severely devastated by Stuka

Koch's next shot captured Oberleutnant Kunz's Panzer '200' approaching an apartment complex near the intersection of the railway line and Plekhanovskaya Street, a major north-south thoroughfare that joined the Zadonsk highway north of the city. Point vehicle is '212', the deputy platoon leader of Leutnant Fritz Heller's 1. Zug.
(BA Bild 101I-216-0436-06A)

A small group of infantrymen has moved up to '212', obviously happy to see the panzers. The positioning of this picture by Sautter in the sequence of his and Koch's photos; the palpable relief on the men's faces, and the presence of 5cm PaK anti-tank guns (one can be seen behind the group) are all strong indications that these men do not belong to the force's own infantry. They are more likely members of the 24. Panzer-Division who have reached this position from the other side of the city. (BA Bild 101I-216-431-30)

The tall apartment block still stands but today sandwiched in between two new buildings. (Sergey Popov)

attacks. The closer we got to the city centre, the more-ghostly the picture became. Downed wires sometimes blocked our path. Several times machine-gun fire flared up so that we had to crouch behind the panzers, but the forward barrels replied quickly and decisively. Then we drove along the north-south axis, the main boulevard and business street of the city [Plekhanovskaya Street]. The Stukas did the greatest damage here. Then the street wound down to the bottom. The road was narrow, the houses not so high. We must be approaching the river quarter. Suddenly there was a halt. The leading vehicle had encountered a large bomb crater that blocked the street. The panzers couldn't continue, so we jumped down and proceeded on foot. In the darkness we recognised that we were facing a very steep descent down the street. The river was probably at the bottom. A reconnaissance troop went towards the river. The street ended and before us lay a meadow. It was a pitch-black night. A few minutes later the patrol returned and reported that the Voronezh river flowed 150 metres away. We were the first to reach the objective.'

This bold penetration, strengthened throughout the night by more companies, spelled disaster to the Soviets as it blocked elements of Major-General Ivan Chernyakhovsky's 18th Tank Corps

None of the old buildings on Donbasskaya Street remain, high-rise developments having taken their place. (Sergey Popov)

The same infantrymen gather around '212' and its dismounted crew. The star attached to the webbing of the man closest to camera may mean he is wearing it as the leader in a forthcoming night patrol, thus making him clearly visible to his comrades following behind. The casual attitude of both the panzer crews and infantrymen appears to indicate that there was no Soviet resistance in the immediate vicinity. The 125th Regiment of the NKVD Railway Services was responsible for defending Voronezh's train stations, so the lack of resistance suggests they had fled. (BA Bild 101I-216-0436-08A)

With the infantrymen having shoved aside the anti-tank obstacles, Panzer '212' cautiously moves northwards past the Voroshilovskaya Polyclinic (marked [B] on the town plan on page 19) towards a T-34 (hidden by the building on the left) sitting askew on an embankment of the ramp to the Plekhanovskaya Street viaduct across the railway. The T-34 and another T-60 had been knocked out by the infantry's 5cm anti-tank guns. (BA Bild 101I-216-0436-12)

Trees mask the view of the polyclinic – today City Clinical Hospital No. 3 – but part of the building's small triangular roof is visible above the trees on the left. (Sergey Popov)

that had been released from Stavka Reserve on July 4 and had moved into the city from the south the previous day. One of its formations, Lieutenant-Colonel Isaak Eisenberg's 110th Tank Brigade, was aware that panzers were present, yet after being evicted from the barracks by Rittmeister von Knebel-Doberitz's men, it still stumbled into an ambush at the Y-junction of Koltsovskaya and 20-letiya Oktyabrya Streets. During the wild nocturnal mêlée, Wachtmeister Siegfried Freyer and his Panzer IV '434' of the 4. Schwadron of Panzer-Regiment 24 knocked out 11 tanks (nine T-34s and two T-60s):

> 'On July 7, I took up position with my Panzer IV long-barrel at an important crossroads in Voronezh, well camouflaged in a garden next to a house. In front of the panzer was a wooden fence, covering us from view from the street. Our orders were to support our panzer grenadiers who were attempting to clear the town, and to protect

Kunz's men spent the night on Bolshaya Streletskaya Street, a cobbled road running along the sloping Strelets Ravine leading down to the west bank of the Voronezh river. The panzer in the foreground of this picture by Koch is '213' from the 1. Zug. While four members of each tank crew slept, the fifth kept watch. Peace reigned during the night. On the morning of July 8, Kunz's company rolled north out of the city to join the rest of Panzer-Abteilung 103 near the airfield on Voronezh's northern outskirts. In the background is the Seeking of the Lost Church. (BA Bild 101-216-0436-31A)

Many of the original houses still stand on Bolshaya Streletskaya Street though the landmark church on its corner with Vyborgskaya Street is long gone. Having been badly damaged during the war, the ruined temple was later turned into a multi-storey residential building. Then, in the early 1960s, rumours spread among believers of the miraculous appearance of an image of the Virgin Mary on an altar that had been uncovered. Pilgrimages to the site began but, despite a petition, the authorities evicted the residents and blew up the remains. A brand-new gated community now occupies the site. (Sergey Popov)

them from enemy tanks. During the day, our only problems came from scattered Russian troops, but the actions between friend and foe in the town kept us on our toes. It was a hot day but we didn't realise that the evening was going to be even hotter. At about 2000 hours, a T-34 appeared from a side street to our left and attempted to get past us at high speed. It was followed by a column of about 30 more tanks and we had to prevent this break-out. We engaged them in quick succession and knocked out the first three T-34s, then our gunner Unteroffizier Alfons Fischer reported: "The gun is jammed!" Our gun was new and had had some teething troubles because every second or third round the empty shell-case got stuck in the breech. Our driver, Unteroffizier

While Kunz's men were securing their overnight billets, a scene of high drama was playing out a few kilometres away. In the afternoon of July 7, three rifle squadrons of Schützen-Regiment 21, supported by a panzer company, squeezed the 110th Tank Brigade out of the Chizhov barracks complex located in the military township. Towards dusk, an estimated 36 Soviet tanks broke out towards the city centre. The German riflemen reported this escape by radio, enabling an ambush to be set up. Wachtmeister Siegfried Freyer and his long-barrel Panzer IV '434' from the 3. Zug of the 4. Schwadron of Panzer-Regiment 24 was deployed at the Y-junction formed by 20-letiya Oktyabrya Street and the dog-legged Koltsovskaya Street (see the town plan on page 19). Freyer positioned his panzer behind a wooden fence, facing south, and in the subsequent night action knocked out 11 of the Soviet tanks – an extraordinary feat that won him the Knight's Cross. No photos of the nocturnal engagement exist but the aftermath was recorded by numerous Kriegsberichter and anyone else with a camera. This is the view looking south down 20-letiya Oktyabrya from Koltsovskaya. Visible are six T-34s and two T-60s.

Wilhelm Schmidt, and I jumped out of the panzer, screwed together the barrel cleaner and with it pushed the casing out of the breech. The next Russian tank fired wildly and wounded our loader Gefreiter Arnold Groll in the head. We pulled him out of the panzer and our radioman, Gefreiter Heinrich Müller, took his place to help operate our weapon. We fired repeatedly and kept on hitting targets. We had to grab the barrel cleaner a few more times and push out the jammed

Freyer occupied the position where the trees and apartment block on the far left now stand. This location restricted his field of fire and reduced range to less than 100 metres, but kept his panzer out of the line of fire for the maximum amount of time. (Sergey Popov)

Lieutenant-Colonel Isaak Eisenberg's 110th Tank Brigade came rolling along Krasnoznamonnaya (Red Banner) Street, then turned left into 20-letiya Oktyabrya Street, fully aware that German armour was in the area. Their combat journal states that 'by 1800 hours on July 7, the enemy had assembled up to a battalion of medium tanks along Koltsovskaya Street and installed anti-tank guns along Kirova Street and other streets leading to the Cherniavskiy bridge.' With this knowledge, Eisenberg chose to escape under the cover of night. However, his force ran straight into Freyer's ambush, the darkness suddenly erupting in a welter of muzzle flashes, sparks and flames, and the metallic thud of solid shot puncturing armour. The Soviet drivers panicked, one T-34 ramming the back of another and scrabbling up onto its engine deck, and another colliding with a T-60 and slewing it across the road. (Jason Mark)

The two T-34s on the left in the top picture have their turrets at six o'clock position (towards Freyer's location), but the one seen here is facing the opposite direction. In the background are another T-34 and two T-60s, making a total of seven T-34s and four T-60s. The sum of 11 corroborates Freyer's account, but Panzer-Regiment 24's order of the day incorrectly breaks that figure down to nine T-34s and two T-60s. (Jason Mark)

Normally this street is full of traffic but Sergey took his comparisons on a Sunday morning to match the emptiness of the wartime photos. (Sergey Popov)

shells and then quickly take cover. The Russians shredded the fence in front of us with their fire, but didn't hit our panzer. We, however, hit 11 enemy tanks, the only time they got past us was when our gun jammed. The engagement lasted about 20 minutes, by then, 11 enemy tanks were on fire in front of us, the flames and explosions giving the place an eerie appearance. That is how the rest of our Schwadron found us, despite the darkness.'

Generalleutnant Henrici, commander of the 16. Infanterie-Division (mot.), was ordered to relieve the 24. Panzer-Division. His division crossed the Don over the bridge at Yunevka but the attack into the city by Oberst Alexander Vial's Infanterie-Regiment 60 scheduled for the pre-noon hours of July 7 was postponed because not all elements had closed up. Eventually, two battalions, supported by anti-tank guns, self-propelled guns and artillery, moved off at 1700 hours toward the large forest south-west of Voronezh. The II. Bataillon (Major

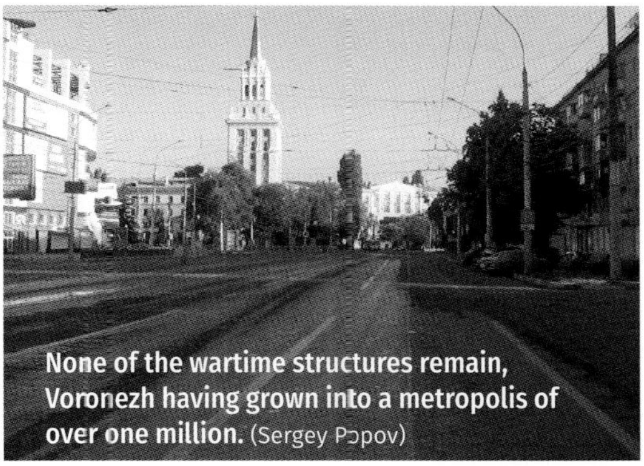

None of the wartime structures remain, Voronezh having grown into a metropolis of over one million. (Sergey Popov)

The Soviet view of Freyer's ambush. Panzer '434' was hidden behind the fence seen demolished in the middle distance on the right. Freyer reported that 'the Russians shredded the fence in front of us with their fire, but didn't hit our panzer.' An explanation can be found in the June 6 entry of 110th Tank Brigade's combat journal: 'There were no anti-tank shells, generally there were just five fragmentation shells per tank and in some tanks there were no shells at all.' (Jason Mark)

Another view of the T-34 whose driver kept spinning his tracks so desperately that he clawed away parts of the leading T-34 and churned the rear part of his tank into the asphalt road surface. Note that the T-60 that stood alongside and the one that was pushed sideways by the T-34 on the right have both gone: all four knocked-out light tanks were dragged to Koltsovskaya Street to form a barricade. (Colin Nicol)

The same view from the north-west corner of Koltsovskaya Street. The western extension of Koltsovskaya was renamed Voroshilova Street after the war. (Sergey Popov)

Otto Lindner) reached the hill 1.5 kilometres north of the Eierwäldchen (Egg Copse) at 1830 hours, but its sister battalion went to ground under ferocious defensive fire. However, following a rocket barrage, the I. Bataillon surged forward and likewise reached the hill. Supporting artillery knocked out two counter-attacking T-34s. Despite failing light, the regiment was ordered to comb through the city and relieve elements of the 24. Panzer-Division holding position along the city's eastern edge by 0500 hours the next morning, but Oberst Vial refused because of the fierce resistance and the expected bitter house-to-house fighting. He stated that the attack would only commence the next morning with panzer support.

With Division's permission, Vial ordered Panzer-Abteilung 116 to move its panzers into the city to support his infantry despite protests by its commander, Major Johann-Matthias Graf von der Schulenberg. Two panzer groups were formed: Oberleutnant Wilfried Palm with the 2. and 4. Kompanien (eight Panzer IIIs and four Panzer IVs) supported the I. Bataillon of Infanterie-Regiment 60 on the left, and Oberleutnant Friedrich Stölting with 13 Panzer IIIs of the 3. Kompanie and three Panzer IVs from the 4. Kompanie went with the II. Bataillon on the right. Schulenberg stressed that the panzer groups not be splintered and that infantrymen advance ahead of the panzers.

Kampfgruppe Vial's attack into Voronezh began at 0745 hours on July 8. Not until the city fringe was reached did the I. Bataillon and Panzergruppe

The prominent water tower on Koltsovskaya Street was toppled during the German occupation of the city. Residential apartments erected in the 1950s and 1960s now occupy the site. (Sergey Popov)

In their death throes, these three T-34s effectively blocked the main arc of Freyer's fire and enabled others to escape the death zone. Instead of veering north-east along Koltsovskaya Street as planned, the column turned west and found refuge amongst the huts north of the barracks. Eisenberg's brigade did not escape its fate for long: at the end of July 8, the 18th Tank Corps recorded in its combat journal that '110th Tank Brigade continued to escape encirclement while losing all available tanks'. Eisenberg and his Chief-of-Staff Lieutenant-Colonel Aleksey Payzanskiy escaped but four other staff officers did not, including the brigade's commissar (Senior Battalion Commissar Ivan Paliy) and chief of brigade HQ, Major Belichev. The survivors gathered in woodlands north of Maklok, a village north-east of Voronezh. (Colin Nicol)

On July 23, 1942, during a break in the fighting, Oberst Gustav-Adolf Riebel and Major Hild-Wilfried von Winterfeld, commander of Panzer-Regiment 24 and its I. Abteilung respectively, awarded Freyer the Ritterkreuz in a small ceremony in the village of Krasnaya Zvezda, while the rest of the crew were recognised for their bravery with the Iron Cross First Class. It was a rare feat for an entire crew to wear this decoration. 'In the name of the regiment', wrote Riebel in an Order of the Day, 'I wish to express my congratulations to Wachtmeister Freyer for his high war decoration. The regiment views with pride and pleasure our Knight's Cross bearer and wishes him further success.' (L-R): Major von Winterfeld, Wachtmeister Freyer, Unteroffizier Alfons Fischer (gunner), Unteroffizier Wilhelm Schmidt (driver) and Gefreiter Heinrich Müller (radioman). Gefreiter Arnold Groll (loader) missed the ceremony because he was in hospital having his wounds treated. (Jason Mark)

The Chizhovskiy Bridgehead Memorial Complex (left), dedicated to the Red Army soldiers who formed a bridgehead across the Voronezh river in August-September 1942, now stands sentinel at the city's south-eastern entrance. (Sergey Popov)

Informed that they would be relieved by the 16. Infanterie-Division, elements of the 24. Panzer-Division began leaving Voronezh during the night and early morning of July 8. With combat still simmering in the industrial district and barracks area, the safest route out of the city was to the south. During its two days of fighting (July 7-8), the division had suffered 125 casualties: two officers and 36 NCOs/men killed, four officers and 81 other ranks wounded, and two men missing. Here, an SdKfz 250 half-track of Kradschützen-Abteilung 4 carefully negotiates the cobbled slope of 20-letiya Oktyabrya Street. Baltiyskiy Alley, the small side street seen in the picture on page 15, is just behind the photographer.
(BA Bild 101-748-0081G-09)

Palm run into frantic resistance from T-34s, T-60s and masses of anti-tank rifles. Soviet tanks deployed skilfully, flanking the streets from hidden positions and throttling progress. Despite promises, German infantry clustered behind their armoured shepherds. The panzers bypassed some tanks and in this manner shot up six T-34s and two T-60s, but Red Army soldiers then began reporting all panzer movements, preventing any further side-step manoeuvres and causing the first panzer casualties: the turrets of two Panzer IVs were jammed by anti-tank rifle strikes, while three Panzer IIIs were lightly damaged by tank fire, which rendered all temporarily non-operational. While shelling a factory near the military barracks, Oberleutnant Palm's Panzer IV '400' was struck in the turret by a concealed T-34 and burned instantly. Palm died of his injuries. Any further advance augured little success, so the panzers pulled back.

The right Kampfgruppe with Stölting's panzers only needed to overcome a

Arriving with the 16. Infanterie-Division were two new photographers, Kriegsberichter Kempe and Gregor of Propaganda-Kompanie OBdH (Oberbefehlshaber des Heeres) and Propaganda-Kompanie 694 respectively. Early on the morning of July 8, Kempe pictured the crew of a 5cm PaK anti-tank gun in defilade position on the sandy verge half-way down 20-letiya Oktyabrya Street. In the distance is a T-34 that was disabled two days earlier. A gunner from the 24. Panzer-Division described the difficulty of engaging enemy tanks from such a position: 'Our anti-tank gun slipped back at least one and a half metres and had to be re-aimed after every shot because the gun spades found no real purchase in the soft and damp sand.' The gun crew seen in this picture itself destroyed a tank at 2030 hours in the evening, as Oberfähnrich Saborowski from the 7. Kompanie of Infanterie-Regiment 60 of the 16. Infanterie-Division reports: 'Two T-34s suddenly appeared from the rear. After about 200 metres, one ran over mines placed in front of the bridge and burned there after a mighty detonation. The second received a PaK hit on the right track and lost it. Nevertheless, the tank rolled on and fired its machine guns and cannon into my platoon until it hit the embankment. One of the crew got out. I took him prisoner and had one of my messengers guard him. Then I dealt with the bogged tank with hand-grenades from about 20 metres away because two more tanks on the other side of the Voronezh river provided cover fire for the stuck tank. In order to avoid further losses, I grabbed two explosive charges. Regardless of my wounded knees and enemy fire, I jumped onto the tank from behind and placed an explosive charge on it. The first charge did not set the tank on fire, so I prepared a second one. I put it behind the turret. Following a powerful detonation, the hatch was torn off and a burning crewman hurled from the turret. Immediately afterwards, the tank burned brightly and the ammunition detonated.' (BA Bild 101I-748-0081G-1[illegible])

Standing almost on the same spot, PK Gregor pictured passenger cars and motorbikes of the 16. Infanterie-Division driving up the same incline. Its Infanterie-Regiment 156 had begun relieving Schützen-Regiment 21 on the city's south-eastern sector on July 7: the II. Bataillon replaced the riflemen in the central city, the III. Bataillon secured to the east in the southern part of Voronezh, and the I. Bataillon held position along the Voronezh river down to its confluence with the Don. (NIOD 16772)

Looking north up the ascending avenue today. (Sergey Popov)

Gregor next pictured men of Infanterie-Regiment 156 marching past the knocked-out T-34. A column of Panzer IIs from Panzer-Regiment 24 idles at the top of the road. This section of 20-letiya Oktyabrya Street was ill-suited for tanks: the elevated ground along both sides formed a defile, while at the bottom the road headed onto a long, exposed causeway that ran across meadowland to the Voronezh river bridge.

'Voronezh, City of Military Glory', reads the slogan on the left. This status was conferred to the city by President of the Russian Federation Vladimir Putin on February 16, 2008.
(Sergey Popov)

solitary plucky Soviet tank before it reached its objective, the southern Voronezh road bridge.

At 0900 hours, the 16. Infanterie-Division's second regiment, Infanterie-Regiment 156 led by Oberstleutnant Johannes Eisermann, reported that its II. Bataillon had reached the railway station from the south-east. Because Kampfgruppe Vial had made good progress, its supporting artillery changed position into the city. At 1330 hours, the I. Bataillon of Infanterie-Regiment 60 encountered stubborn resistance on the north-eastern city limits and was temporarily pinned down. The regiment's III. Bataillon, held in reserve until this point, moved off from the south with the task of clearing the city up to the railway line, but it too ran into obstinate resistance and tanks in the industrial area. Due to the tank threat, particularly at major intersections, anti-tank guns were moved into position for the night.

Once elements of the 16. Infanterie-Division made contact, Infanterie-Regiment 8 of Schlömer's 3. Infanterie-Division shuffled northward into a warren of allotments and shacks and started setting up eastward-

As the men of the 16. Infanterie-Division prepared to launch their attack on the morning of July 8, they were surprised to hear a special radio report about the fall of Voronezh, a broadcast that proved premature. Pre-battle reconnaissance revealed powerful Soviet forces, including 30 to 40 tanks, in the industrial area west of the city, around the railway station, on the airfield and tank training ground, and in the military township known as Red or Military Town N. I. Muralov. This T-34 stranded in a bomb crater on Krasnoznamonnaya Street most likely blundered into it during 110th Tank Brigade's nocturnal break-out from the Chizhov barracks. Aerial photos reveal a string of bomb craters – at least five – along this stretch of tramway. (NIOD 16783)

The No. 2 tram, connecting the military town with the city, ran along Krasnoznamonnaya Street until 2009 when the rails were lifted. (Sergey Popov)

facing defences. The rest of Schlömer's division began shifting the Nordriegelstellung (northern blocking position) northward onto higher ground. At 0800 hours, Major Günther Mollenhauer's II. Bataillon of Infanterie-Regiment 29, supported by the tanks of Hauptmann Haen's 1. Kompanie of Panzer-Abteilung 103, attacked over exposed ground towards the village of Podgornoye, held by weak remnants of Lieutenant-Colonel Ivan Ulitin's 232nd Rifle Division. Despite inflicting considerable casualties on Mollenhauer's infantry with a few machine guns, the depleted Siberians could not hold back the onslaught and retreated. Shortly afterwards, movement was seen in the woods two kilometres to the north. Substantial Soviet forces had arrived, including elements of Chernyakhovsky's 18th Tank

Corps (four tank battalions and a motorised infantry battalion), later joined by sub-units of Major-General Pyotr Zykov's 121st Rifle Division and Lieutenant-Colonel Sergey Styzika's 14th Tank Brigade. Major Mollenhauer reported:

> 'Tanks rolled up, but then pulled back after the first ones were knocked out. The infantry attack came in on a slope that fell gently towards the battalion's position. The battalion waited until the Russians were within 200 metres before opening fire. Then all weapons fired at once and smashed back the attack with heavy losses [for the Russians].'

Styzika's 14th Tank Brigade lost nine Lend-Lease Mark III Valentines and four BT-7s, and had 11 men killed – including two battalion commanders (Major Pyotr Fomichev and Captain Bogatyuk) – and 18 wounded.

German forces crossed the Zadonsk highway and infiltrated the botanical garden and campus of the agricultural college on the north-eastern outskirts of the city. A new defensive front was established, the 88mm and anti-tank guns forming a Panzerriegel (anti-tank barrier) behind the infantry while a mobile panzer reserve stood by in the forest east of Podkletnoye.

SOVIET BREAK-OUT ATTEMPT

In the pre-dawn gloom of July 9, the remaining Soviet tanks inside Voronezh launched a desperate break-out bid, attempting to escape in two different directions, eastwards to the city's southern road bridge at Monastyrshchenka, and southwards to the Don bridge at Yunevka and the ferry site over the Voronezh at Yakovlevka, the latter two sites being well beyond the city. Bursting out of the industrial area in several groups, Colonel Vasili Konovalov's 181st Tank Brigade, followed by lorries filled with soldiers, charged south along the city streets, about a dozen tanks with mounted infantry, firing from all barrels, broke through the ranks of the I. Bataillon of Infanterie-Regiment 60 and rolled over Vial's regimental command post. Most of the tanks were destroyed inside the city limits, just three managing to pass through and continue southwards. However, before they got to any of the bridges or ferries, they encountered Infanterie-Regiment 156. Oberstleutnant Eisermann, its commander, was alerted by gun-fire. One T-34 was knocked out directly in front of his command post, another came to grief on mines on the Monastyrshchenka bridge. The crews, some wounded, were captured. Prisoners asserted that these tanks were tasked with breaking through to the south or south-west in order to facilitate the escape of about 100 infantrymen. While some trucks were captured, others hurtled toward the ferry site at Shilovo, where their men abandoned them and swam the Voronezh. A single T-34 made it to the Yunevka bridge and surprised its garrison. A Russian officer dismounted under 2cm Flak fire and guided his tank onto the narrow bridge, but he fell, wounded. An 88mm gun on the southern bank then struck the tank, causing it to reverse in panic and run over the wounded officer. Its journey ended when it careered down a slope.

At 7.45 a.m. on July 8, preceded by an artillery barrage on the barracks and airfield hangars, Infanterie-Regiment 60 moved off to attack the city from the south-west. In support were two mixed groups from Panzer-Abteilung 116, until then held in reserve in woodlands near Malyshevo but now called into action with the 2. Kompanie and part of the 4. Kompanie under Oberleutnant Wilfried Palm on the left and the 3. Kompanie with the remainder of the 4. Kompanie under Oberleutnant Friedrich Stölting on the right. Kriegsberichter Sonntag went with Stölting's group and he pictured a Panzer III from the 3. Kompanie driving along cobbled Novo Slobodskaya Street, just short of the intersection with 20-letiya Oktyabrya Street. Palm's group encountered fierce opposition and lost several tanks, while Stölting had an easier time, as revealed in his combat report: 'The company was subordinated to the II. Bataillon of Infanterie-Regiment 60 with 13 Panzer IIIs and three Panzer IVs. The infantry battalion advanced in its attack lane with two companies in the forward line. My company was divided into three groups. Each light platoon was allocated one Panzer IV. Leutnant Endres led the left Panzergruppe, Leutnant Schaumann the right, while Leutnant Kinzer's was in reserve. Upon setting off, Leutnant Endres's group received fire from enemy tanks and anti-tank guns. Panzer '311' (Leutnant Endres) was hit and damaged by an anti-tank gun. Endres and his group were withdrawn behind a rise in the ground. Leutnant Kinzer was moved up from the right and took over the task of Leutnant Endres, who remained with the reserve group. The battalion progressed along its attack lane without enemy contact to the objective (eastern edge of the city). By listening in to the radio messages of Oberleutnant Palm's group, my company was aware of the resistance there. I pivoted Leutnant Endres's reserve group leftward in order to strike the resistance nest holding up Palm from the south-east, but after discussions with Oberleutnant Palm via radio, this intervention was not desired.' Shortly afterwards, Palm's Panzer IV was struck and he was fatally wounded. After reaching the eastern edge of the city, Stölting's panzers turned off and reached the southern bridge without incident. The battalion commander, Major Johann-Matthias von der Schulenberg, then ordered Stölting to concentrate his platoons along 20-letiya Oktyabrya Street, about two kilometres north of the bridge, and so they pulled back to the 'Park of the Living and the Dead', their vehicles having barely any fuel left. Panzer-Abteilung 116 only operated in Voronezh for one day, but even that was too much for Major von der Schulenberg: 'The old principle has once again been proven: panzers have no place in city fighting.' The battalion set in march to Ustye in the evening, having lost seven Panzer IIIs and three Panzer IVs. (BA Bild 101I-79-3124-11A)

Novo Slobodskaya Street was renamed Moiseyeva Street in 1967 in honour of Aleksei Moiseyev, a Bolshevik coup leader shot by the White Guards in 1919. (Sergey Popov)

In one week, Konovalov's 181st Tank Brigade, lost 35 T-34s and 13 T-60s, as well as 72 dead, 22 wounded (evacuated to hospital) and 460 missing. Amongst the casualties were 80 officers (16 dead, seven wounded and 57 missing). The other formation of the 18th Tank Corps deployed in the city, Eisenberg's 110th Tank Brigade, had lost 33 T-34s and 13 T-60s, while 11 T-34s and eight T-60s were evacuated for repairs. Personnel losses were 40 dead, 83 wounded and 235 missing.

North of the city, two Soviet infantry regiments attacked out of the forest at dawn, striking the I. Bataillon of Infanterie-Regiment 8 and Haen's company of panzers. Twenty-seven Soviet tanks were knocked out. Ten tanks pushed along the railway into the city and suddenly appeared in the rear of the regiment's II. Bataillon. Four of them were blasted by self-propelled 7.62cm Marders of Panzerjäger-Abteilung 3.

SOVIET COUNTER-OFFENSIVE

On July 10, Generalleutnant Oskar Blümm's 57. Infanterie-Division crossed the Don near the village of Malyshevo, just north of the Yunevka bridge, and began relieving Henrici's 16. Infanterie-Division in the southern part of the bridgehead. Meanwhile, in the northern part, on the front of the 3. Infanterie-Division, the Soviet 476th Separate Tank Battalion moved against Podgornoye with its 15 KV-1s. Haen's panzer company knocked out seven of the behemoths but paid a steep price: eight dead and four wounded. An armour-piercing round took off Oberfeldwebel Willy Tiemann's head, while Feldwebel August Aretz's panzer was shot into flames: just one crew member survived. A KV punctured Feldwebel Josef Mühlmichl's Panzer III from the side. The gunner was killed instantly, Mühlmichl's feet were torn off and he bled to death within a few minutes.

Despite destroying 64 enemy tanks between July 6 and 10, the staff of the 3. Infanterie-Division assessed all of these attacks as probes and therefore expected a major assault by the tank corps assembling in the woods. When this large-scale attack failed to eventuate on July 11, the German command decided to take the railway bridge four kilometres north of the city, but was forestalled by a powerful Soviet artillery response. Due to the tense situation, the planned relief of Schlömer's division by Generalleutnant Dietrich Kraiss's 168. Infanterie-Division was delayed until the following day.

German intelligence was spot on, the Red Army was indeed preparing a major assault. This offensive was entrusted to Lieutenant-General Antoniuk's 60th Army, fresh from reserve. Colonel Pavel Kochetkov's 161st Rifle Division, supported by Colonel Fedor Korol's 111th Tank Brigade, the 476th Separate Tank Battalion and four companies of heavy KVs, was ordered to advance towards the Podgornoye workers settlement. Attacking into the north-eastern outskirts of Voronezh were Colonel Mikhail Mikeladze's 195th and Zykov's 121st Rifle Divisions, each supported by a tank brigade. Three German infantry battalions therefore faced three fresh Soviet divisions.

Fortunately, the building at No. 88 is one of the few on 20-letiya Oktyabrya to have escaped redevelopment since the war. (Sergey Popov)

A self-propelled 2cm Flak gun of Infanterie-Regiment 60 that accompanied Stölting's column drives south along 20-letiya Oktyabrya Street, pictured by Sonntag. Soviet aircraft rarely appeared over the city – the 24. Panzer-Division downed two on July 7 – so the rapid-firing guns were mostly deployed against enemy strongholds. Oberstleutnant Johannes Eisermann, the commander of Infanterie-Regiment 156, recalled that all day on July 8 'there was frequent street and house combat against fiercely defended resistance nests. This fighting was very well supported by our self-propelled 2cm Flak platoon.' Each motorised infantry regiment possessed one company of light flak. (BA Bild 101I-79-3124-17A)

After preparatory rocket and artillery fire, the German defenders heard a guttural 'uraaaaa' swell from the woods at 1000 hours on July 12. The Soviet attack came in three wedges: the first along the railway struck the I. Bataillon of Infanterie-Regiment 8 with its full weight; the second down the highway pushed into the regiment's III. Bataillon while the third raced towards the II. Bataillon of Infanterie-Regiment 29 in Podgornoye. Swirling dust stained the sun-bleached sky. The 195th and 121st Rifle Divisions, supported by 26 tanks, overran German infantry positions, but by the afternoon 88s had knocked out 14 of the tanks and the attack was repulsed. The III. Bataillon of Infanterie-Regiment 8 parried the attack down the highway.

In the west, Hauptmann Ewald von Stünzner, commander of the 3. Kompanie of Panzer-Abteilung 103, had positioned his seven long-barrel Panzer IVs amongst Podgornoye's shacks, his western flank protected by an oxbow lake. In the rush to Podgornoye, the riflemen of the 161st Rifle

Division were overtaken by the 111th Tank Brigade. Leading the way were KV-1s and T-34s, followed by a second wave with Mark II Matildas and T-34s with mounted infantry. The Germans counted 40 tanks. Hauptmann von Stünzner opened fire at close range, buffeting the Soviet tanks with a squall of projectiles. Several brewed up, others veered away into a minefield, while the rest, together with the riflemen, retreated north to the safety of the woods. Soviet artillery pummelled the village and another attack began, this time with 26 tanks. Fighting surged until 1400 hours, then the Soviets gave up after losing 34 tanks. Stünzner suffered zero combat losses and secured himself the Knight's Cross.

Soviet losses were ghastly: the 161st Rifle Division had lost a staggering 574 men killed, 1,262 wounded and 144 missing between July 12 and 14, including 40 dead officers on July 12 alone. Seven officers from the 111th Tank Brigade were killed on the 12th.

On July 13 the Soviets repeated their breakthrough attempt with weaker forces. Stukas intervened from 0300 hours. Stünzner's 3. Kompanie was replaced by Haen's 1. Kompanie, which knocked out ten tanks during the day. Even though combat had not yet concluded, Schlömer's division was relieved by the 168. Infanterie-Division in the evening. Panzer-Abteilung 103 and Panzerjäger-Abteilung 3 remained for another 24 hours.

Responsibility for holding Voronezh now fell to the purely infantry formations of Korpsgruppe Blümm (57., 75. and 323. Infanterie-Divisions) under Generalleutnant Blümm, the commander of the 57. Division. Heavy fighting – exclusively German defence against Soviet tank-heavy attacks – continued until July 24. Small-scale combat continued thereafter, punctuated occasionally by large-scale probing attacks that resulted in bloody Soviet losses, but front lines around Voronezh ossified as focus shifted southward to the mighty battles in the Don bend, Stalingrad and the Caucasus. The men of General der Infanterie Hans von Salmuth's 2. Armee occupied Voronezh for the next five months.

FATAL DELAY?

The German advance to Voronezh was no doubt an emphatic victory that secured an eastern anchor point for a north-facing defensive line, but Hitler was convinced that the week-long delay resulting from the commitment of armoured forces to capture the city had derailed the timetable for 'Blau', squandered opportunities to eliminate major Red Army formations and fatally deferred the capture of Stalingrad.

On July 5, Hitler had permitted Generalfeldmarschall von Bock to continue with the occupation of Voronezh but attempted to stimulate the offensive by bisecting his Heeresgruppe Süd into two formations – Heeresgruppen A and B, in order to attain widely spaced objectives, namely Stalingrad and the Caucasus – and shifting the main effort southward. General Paulus of the 6. Armee was ordered to send General der Kavallerie Georg Stumme's XXXX. Panzer-Korps

A perfect comparison by Sergey, looking eastwards into Kirova Street. (Sergey Popov)

Set up at the crossroads of Novo Slobodskaya/Kirova and 20-letiya Oktyabrya Streets, the crew of 8.8cm Flak gun *Berta* peer into the afternoon sun, ready to intercept Soviet tanks approaching from the west. Their gun shield boasts an impressive kill tally of 11 aircraft, 40 tanks and 15 bunkers, though it is likely that this score sheet represents the entire four-gun battery. Photo reporter Karl Hubert Müller-Schwanneke of Propaganda-Kompanie 670, attached to the 2. Armee, took several photos of this gun and its crew, one of which featured on the cover of the Luftwaffe periodical *Der Adler.* The shield-and-oakleaf emblem represents the I. Flak-Korps and the white 'T' shape on the other mudguard probably denotes the flak battalion, though it is unknown which one.

south to link up with the 1. Panzer-Armee near Millerovo, 300 kilometres south of Voronezh, and as soon as Hoth's 4. Panzer-Armee handed responsibility of Voronezh's defence to the 2. Armee, it was to overtake the 6. Armee.

Problems arose when Golikov's Voronezh Front committed Major-General Alexander Liziukov's 5th Tank Army to strike Hoth's long and vulnerable northern flank west of Voronezh. An attack by a single tank corps (Major-General Pavel Rotmistrov's 7th Tank Corps) on July 6 swelled to three tank corps (Major-General Andrei Kravchenko's 2nd Tank Corps and Major-General Aleksei Popov's 11th Tank Corps joining the fray) two days later. Tank clashes raged along this defensive front between Livny and Voronezh for over a week. Von Langermann's XXIV. Panzer-Korps staved off the Soviet thrusts and even counter-attacked with the 11. Panzer-Division on July 12, clobbering the 2nd and 7th Tank Corps and effectively terminating Liziukov's attack.

Further down Kirova Street, Kriegsberichter Koch pictured motorcyclists from the 13. Kompanie (infantry gun) of either Infanterie-Regiment 60 or 156 trying to disentangle a piece of wire wrapped around the rear wheel. The distinctive building in the background is Hotel Voronezh on Ploschad 20-letiya Oktyabrya (20th Anniversary of October Square). At 9.45 a.m. on July 8, the II. Bataillon of Infanterie-Regiment 156 hoisted the red war flag there on what they called the 'town hall turret'.

The 250-room Hotel Voronezh operated from 1940 to 1942 and again from 1951 to 1989. Today, the building houses the Regional Council of Trade Unions. (Sergey Popov)

Between July 6 and 15, the 5th Tank Army suffered nearly 8,000 casualties and lost 341 tanks, including 130 T-34s, 59 KV-1s and 51 Matilda IIs. Their sacrifice, however, had unforeseen and long-term ramifications for the Germans.

Hitler had wanted Hoth's 4. Panzer-Armee sent south immediately after being extracted from Voronezh on July 8, but von Bock was reluctant to release the mobile formations due to 5th Tank Army's counter-offensive. Hoth and von Bock compromised by despatching the XXXXVIII. Panzer-Korps south, but kept the XXIV. Panzer-Korps for another week, a necessary tactical decision that threatened to upset German operational plans. And so began the second phase of 'Blau' on July 9, not with an overwhelming armoured wave formed by Hoth's entire 4. Panzer-Armee, but with a northern pincer comprising just three divisions of Stumme's XXXX. Panzer-

20th Anniversary of October Square attracted a constant stream of visitors, PK photographers heading there even before the city was secured. This photo was taken by Luftwaffe reporter Niermann during 24. Panzer-Division's sweep of the city on the morning of July 7. Six months later, on January 24, 1943, four Soviet armies launched the Voronezh-Kastornoye offensive and soldiers of the 60th Army pushed into the city the next day. Before withdrawing, German forces demolished many government buildings around the square and left behind a soldiers' cemetery on the adjoining Koltsovsky Square (off to the right). The Soviet conquerors hoisted the Red Banner of Victory from a balcony of the Hotel Voronezh.

The square has undergone several name changes in its history. Originally called Equestrian Square, then Starokonnaya, it was renamed 20th Anniversary of October Square in 1937. The statue of Lenin erected in 1940 was removed by the Germans during their occupation. A new monument to Lenin was erected in 1950 and six years later the square received its modern name – Ploschad Lenina (Lenin Square). The colonnaded building is the Voronezh State Opera and Ballet Theatre. (Sergey Popov)

Korps: the 3. and 23. Panzer-Divisions and the 29. Infanterie-Division (mot). It was not until July 12 that Kempf's XXXXVIII. Panzer-Korps (with the 24. Panzer-Division and 16. and Grossdeutschland motorised divisions) rejoined the main southward assault near Nikolayevka and Ostrogozhsk.

Hitler was certain that Red Army formations were fleeing in disarray and that von Bock had missed a golden opportunity to annihilate vast numbers of them. By July 12, Hitler and the OKH believed the Soviets were planning to hold the Millerovo–Kamensk–Shakhtinskii–Rostov line and that it was essential that Hoth break this line as soon as possible. Generaloberst Franz Halder, Chief of the General Staff of the Army, recorded in his diary: 'The Führer expressed his utmost displeasure over the delay in the move to the front of [the divisions] of the 4. Panzer-Armee. He blames the failure on the fact that the 24. Panzer-

Division and the Grossdeutschland, against the Führer's orders, were sent into Voronezh, causing a delay that could have been avoided.'

As such, the OKH issued a new directive: Hoth's 4. Panzer-Armee was to join Heeresgruppe A and proceed towards Kamensk with the objective of engaging and destroying the enemy north of the Don, while Paulus's 6. Armee covered this movement to the east and created the conditions for an advance towards Stalingrad. Bock vehemently disagreed because his armoured formations were being dispersed. Hitler, already agitated by von Bock's hesitation and intransigence, had had enough: he relieved von Bock of command and replaced him with Generaloberst Weichs. New orders issued to both army groups on the evening of July 13 re-oriented the entire offensive southward and south-westward and ultimately set it on course for Stalingrad.

The week-long delay at Voronezh doubtlessly contributed to the failure to seize Stalin's namesake city in a surprise raid.

SOVIET RECAPTURE OF VORONEZH

By mid-January 1943, Voronezh was at the apex of a very long bulge as a result of a succession of Soviet offensives that toppled Axis defences south to north like dominos. First Operation 'Uranus' at Stalingrad from November 19-23, then 'Little Saturn' on the middle Don in mid-December, and lastly the Ostrogozhsk-Rossoshk operation beginning on January 12, 1943, which ripped apart the Hungarian Second Army, the direct southern neighbour of the 2. Armee. The disintegration of the Hungarians prompted the Stavka to hurriedly plan a new attack to encircle and destroy the 2. Armee in the Voronezh area. The Voronezh–Kastornoye operation – the fourth phase of the general Soviet winter offensive of 1942-43 – was implemented by the 13th Army of Lieutenant-General Max Reyter's Bryansk Front and three armies (the 38th, 60th and 40th) of Golikov's Voronezh Front.

On January 24, 1943, the 40th Army (now led by Lieutenant-General Kirill Moskalenko) attacked the underbelly of the 2. Armee's salient and created the impression that the offensive would unfold only along this axis. German intelligence failed to detect the preparations of Pukhov's 13th Army and Lieutenant-General Nikandr Chibisov's 38th Army. The OKH authorised the 2. Armee to withdraw from its exposed positions at Voronezh on January 25, yet the army suffered a catastrophic reverse when the unexpected assaults from the north began. Two of its three corps were encircled when the Soviet pincers met at Kastornoye on January 28. Busting out of the encirclement and retreating westward in the middle of the Russian winter caused considerable losses and the 2. Armee barely escaped destruction, yet its impotence left a weak point in the Axis line that opened the way to Kursk for the Soviets. The entire German southern wing seemed on the point of dissolution. To precipitate a total collapse and force the Germans back to the Dnepr river, the Stavka approved two operations – 'Skachok' (Gallop) and 'Zvezda' (Star) – to liberate the Donbas, Kharkov and Kursk, and shove German forces back over the Dnepr.

The ravages of war left 92 per cent of Voronezh in ruins. This picture was taken from the rear window of a building on 20-letiya Oktyabrya Street looking north-east across the city centre in November 1942. (NIOD 16789)

Large swathes of territory were liberated, as were several major cities – though Kharkov was recaptured by Generalfeldmarschall Erich von Manstein – but the resulting bulge centred upon Kursk set the scene for operations in 1943.

Riflemen of Zykov's 121st Rifle Division (the same formation that had fought in the attack to recapture the city the previous July) entered Voronezh on January 25, 1943. Large detachments immediately began combing the city for 'lone wolves and enemy spies', while teams started clearing obstacles from the streets, bridges and buildings. Recapturing the city cost Zykov just ten dead and 19 wounded. The ghost city lay in ruins with 92 per cent of all of its buildings destroyed. Voronezh was conferred the status of 'City of Military Glory' by President Vladimir Putin on February 16, 2008.

There are two main war memorials in Voronezh city today. One is the Chizhovskiy Bridgehead Memorial on 20-letiya Oktyabrya Street (see page 40), the other is in the Patriots Park along Prospekt Leninskiy (Lenin Avenue) on the east bank of the Voronezh river. Here our photographer Sergey Popov stands in front of the impressive Chizhovskiy memorial. (Sergey Popov)

STALINGRAD

By Mark Holoboski and Alexander Trofimov

IN CLASSIC ACCOUNTS of the Second World War, the Battle for Stalingrad has been viewed as the great turning point of the conflict, which gains even greater interest given the fact that the battle, which came to be synonymous with street fighting and destruction, was never supposed to happen. There

Ever since the start of *After the Battle* back in 1973, we have wanted to do a feature on the battle of Stalingrad – the most-famous and most-crucial battle fought on the Eastern Front, decisive for the outcome of the entire war. However, in all these years, the problems of presenting the story in our customary 'then and now' format seemed insurmountable. Not only was it difficult to find enough photographs that stood a chance of being matched up but, more importantly, we were acutely aware that the city of Stalingrad had been largely destroyed in the months-long struggle and one would need expert knowledge of the rebuilt metropolis (which in 1961 had its name changed to Volgograd) in order to pinpoint the comparisons. So we are therefore immensely fortunate to have established contact with Alexander Trofimov, seen here outside the city's State Panoramic Museum 'Battle of Stalingrad'. Alexander was born in Volgograd in 1970 and has lived there all his life. Ever since he was a youngster, he has been fascinated by the momentous struggle that occurred in his home city and he has spent years studying the details of the ferocious combat that took place there and exploring the battleground – not only in the city proper but also on the wide steppe outside. He knows virtually every corner of the former battlefield and we could not wish to have a better expert to match up the photos of the battle. His photographic contribution to this story is such that our American author, Mark Holoboski, another long-time student of the battle, agreed to share authorship with him. (Alexander Trofimov)

The city that bore Stalin's name was originally named Tsaritsyn. Its roots date back to the late 16th century when a fortress was built near the confluence of the Volga and Tsaritsa rivers to defend the unstable southern border of the country. A small trading settlement soon grew up and this became the nucleus of the town. In the 19th century, the location became an important river port and commercial centre, its population expanding rapidly from 3,000 people in 1807 to 84,000 in 1900. The first railway was constructed to the town in 1862 and the first steel mill opened in 1875. During the Russian Civil War, the city was besieged by counter-revolutionary 'White' forces. The Soviet defenders under Josef Stalin repulsed three assaults, and after the Whites finally captured the city in June 1919, Stalin led a brilliant counter-attack in January 1920, winning a pivotal victory in the revolution. To honour his role in its defence, the city was renamed Stalingrad in 1925. Under Stalin, the city became a centre of heavy industry, its new industrial plants exporting tractors, guns, textiles, timber and chemicals to all parts of the Soviet Union. By 1939 the city of 500,000 inhabitants stretched over 25 kilometres along the Volga's west bank. Representative of the modern metropolis was the Square of Fallen Heroes in the city centre.

certainly was to be an urban fight that year, but much farther north at Leningrad. While the assertion that Stalingrad being the turning point has been the subject of recent debate, with some historians choosing instead to cite the later Battle of Kursk as the definitive loss of German initiative in the East, it cannot be understated that the loss of both Stalingrad and of the German 6. Armee, in the dramatic fashion in which it occurred, was the first true systemic shock to the German leadership, military and citizenry during the conflict. Even more vital to the Allied cause, the battle served as a tremendous morale boost for a resurgent Red Army that had hardly known anything more than defeat and retreat during the previous year and a half. By the time of the surrender of the Stalingrad pocket on the icy morning of February 2, 1943, the once stumbling and off-balance Russian bear was finally awake, and on all fours. The prospect of a Nazi empire in the East dissipated with each quenching ember of the still-glowing ruins of Stalingrad.

In 1942 Stalingrad was a sprawling industrial and transportation hub running for 25 kilometres along the western bank of the Volga river, not dissimilar in shape to that of a question mark. By the time the German 6.

A perfect match, taken by Alex Trofimov seven decades after the battle. (Alexander Trofimov)

The battle of Stalingrad formed one of the decisive turning points in the Second World War. The advance of the German armies to the great city on the Volga in August 1942; the stubborn and heroic defence of the besieged and shell-battered city against overwhelming German superiority by the Soviet 62nd Army in September-November; and the subsequent encirclement and demise of the 6. Armee in the winter of 1942-43, ending in total capitulation on February 2, 1943, decisively turned the scale of the conflict on the Eastern Front. After Stalingrad there could be only one end to the war. Symbolic for the German catastrophe on the Volga is this image of German POWs being marched past one of the most iconic buildings of the struggle: the heavily embattled Grain Elevator in the southern part of the city. (Novosti)

Armee arrived, its population had doubled because of the influx of refugees from the western regions to a total of around 900,000. The city was the location of three of the largest armaments factories in the Soviet Union. In the north there was the pride of Soviet industry, the great Dzerzhinsky Tractor Works, churning out its famed 'chisel-nosed' T-34 tanks in great quantities. Then came the Barrikady Gun Factory laden with artillery barrels while in the south, producing small arms and metal parts, was the Red October Plant.

In transportation terms, being situated on the mighty Volga and, to a lesser extent, on rail lines running to the Caucasus, central Asia, the greater Moscow region and beyond, Stalingrad was indeed an important warehousing and trans-shipment port. Some 30 million tons of goods (timber, oil, coal, grain and heavy industrial products) were moved annually

The advance on Stalingrad began in earnest with the German armies crossing the Don river. Before sunrise on August 21, the LI. Armee-Korps of the 6. Armee launched two amphibious assaults across the Don some 60 kilometres north-west of Stalingrad, the 76. Infanterie-Division on the left establishing a bridgehead near Akimovskiy and the 295. Infanterie-Division on the right another one near Lutchenskiy. Engineers immediately began construction of pontoon bridges at both sites, the idea being to push all three divisions of the XIV. Panzer-Korps – the 16. Panzer-Division and the 3. and 60. Infanterie-Divisions (mot.) – across for the final drive to Stalingrad. The bridge at Lutchenskiy was completed in the afternoon of the 21st and the one at Akimovskiy the following morning. Here panzers of Panzer-Abteilung 103, the tank unit of the 3. Infanterie-Division, cross the span on the 23rd. (Jason Mark)

The locations where armies crossed rivers and built bridges are usually well documented in the unit reports and records, making it relatively easy to find the sites, especially when there are distinctively-shaped ridges lining the river as occurs here near Lutchenskiy. This is the view from the east bank. (Alexander Trofimov)

The battle area between the Don river and Stalingrad. This German intelligence map shows the Soviet defences in front of the city as they appeared on August 3. We have indicated the places that feature in our story.

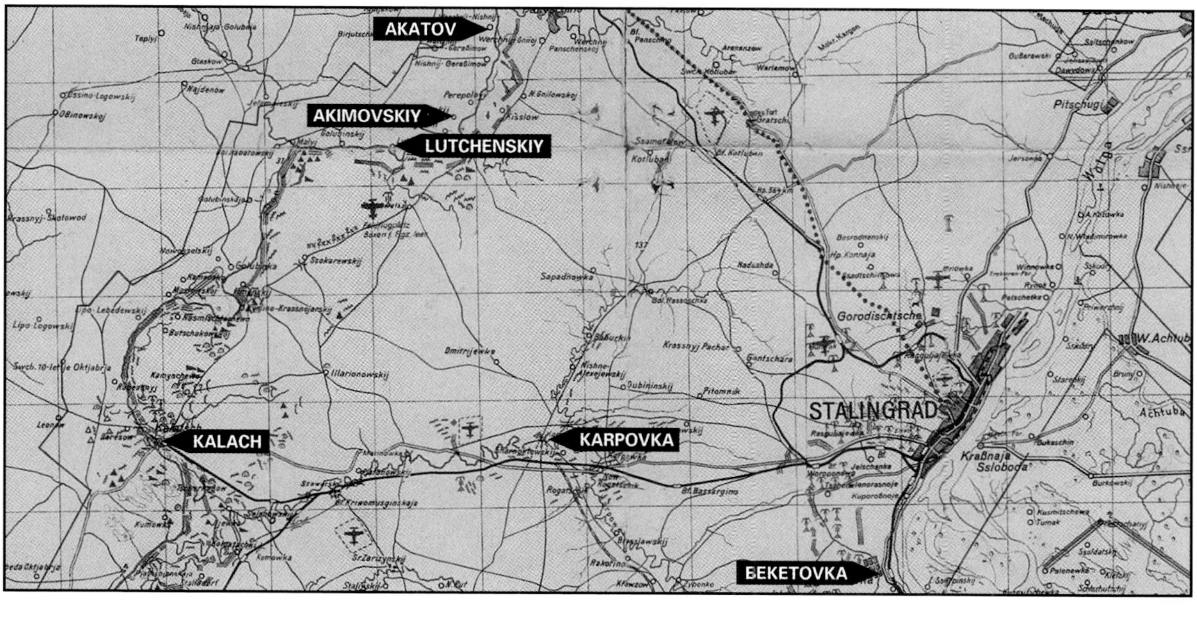

In late August, PK photographer Schüller from Luftwaffe-Kriegsberichter-Kompanie 8 pictured a motorcycle combination on what the Germans called the Donhöhenstrasse (Don Heights Road) on the river's west bank. The sign on the right points to the three bridges across the Don. The northernmost crossing, at Akatov, leading into a bridgehead captured by the 384. Infanterie-Division on August 15-16, was little used, the position being maintained largely to protect the other two bridgeheads further south. All traffic and supplies for the divisions of the XIV. Panzer-Korps fighting east of the Don were channelled through the bridges at Akimovskiy and Lutchenskiy. (BA Bild 101I-454-1079-30)

Normally pictures taken in the endless steppe of Russia stand little chance of being matched up but the sign enabled Alex to locate this one with certainty. This is the old Donhöhenstrasse, looking north at the turn-off to Lutchenskiy (the official Russian name of the village is Luchenskiy). (Alexander Trofimov)

over the Volga during its six ice-free months, and with its network of canals and tributaries, could reach industrial and population centres ranging from the oilfields of the Caucasus to the northern seaports of Leningrad and Archangel. In effect, the Volga connected the White, Black, Baltic, Barents and Caspian Seas, which was strategically vital for such a landlocked country as the Soviet Union. Even more significant to many strategic planners and laymen alike, was the fact that the Volga was the last great natural obstacle to the landmass of Asia, being a mere 150 kilometres from the Russia-Kazakhstan border, and over 2,000 kilometres from Berlin.

Indeed, one of the first panzer crewmen to set foot on the shores of the Volga in late August would later recall:

> 'And then, suddenly, a broad silvery ribbon, the Volga. We knew this was the goal. The ultimate goal of the war maybe. And beyond the Volga,

to the east, we saw the vast deep forests stretching into the horizon shrouded in mystery. And then this boundless view into the expanse of Asia, nothing but forests . . . forests, steppes and endlessness. It was an exciting feeling.'

An old proverb states that 'Russia can only be conquered if the enemy crosses the Volga', and while the notion of setting foot upon Asian soil might have seemed a romantic dream to many, Hitler's true goal for 1942 was to conquer the oilfields in the Soviet Caucasus to the west of the Caspian Sea and south of Stalingrad. As long as German lines advanced close enough to shut down its vast industrial output, the actual occupation of Stalin's city was initially considered by the Führer as being unnecessary.

THE GERMAN 1942 SUMMER OFFENSIVE

Hitler's summer campaign to conquer Caucasian oil began on the morning of June 28, 1942. The plan called for a north-to-south breakthrough of the Soviet defences, staggered over several days.

On the morning of August 23, the 16. Panzer-Division attacked to break out of the Don bridgehead, spearheading the advance of XIV. Panzer-Korps. Bursting through the strong Russian defences, the panzers rolled forward against little opposition and by early afternoon were approaching Stalingrad. A screen of 37 anti-tank guns, emplaced near the northern suburbs of Spartanovka, Rynok and Latashinka (and operated by female gun crews), tried to hold up the advance but was smashed by the panzers and panzergrenadiers in close combat. In the early evening, at 1835 hours, the lead units of the 16. Panzer-Division reached the banks of the Volga just north of the city. Here the crew of an SdKfz 232 heavy armoured car from Kradschützen-Bataillon 16 scours the opposite bank from the high ground overlooking the river. (Jason Mark)

The same spot on the Volga's west bank near Latashinka.
(Alexander Trofimov)

Two days later, on August 25, 75 kilometres to the west, the 71. Infanterie-Division of the XXIV. Panzer-Korps launched yet another assault across the Don river near the town of Kalach. By noon, they had established a large bridgehead and by early evening, despite interruption by Soviet mortar fire, engineers had erected a pontoon bridge, thus opening up a second front against Stalingrad for the 6. Armee. This picture was taken from the west bank. (Jason Mark)

Operation 'Blau I' would be the assault by Generalfeldmarschall Fedor von Bocks's Heeresgruppe Süd. Comprising the 2. Armee, 6. Armee, 4. Panzer-Armee and the Hungarian Second Army, they would emerge from their jump-off positions just east of Kursk and Belgorod and head towards Voronezh and the River Don. Although the 6. Armee, commanded by General der Panzertruppe Friedrich Paulus, was delayed two days due to heavy rain, the Soviet defences were easily cracked and a slow withdrawal began back to the Don, just over 250 kilometres from the front lines.

According to the master plan, 'Blau II' would see the next unit to the south of Paulus – the 1. Panzer-Armee under Generaloberst Ewald von Kleist – begin its drive eastwards from south of Kharkov. It was to link up with Generaloberst Hermann Hoth's 4. Panzer-Armee and Paulus's 6. Armee coming down the west bank of the Don to surround a large Soviet force in an encirclement battle.

Operation 'Blau III' would feature Heeresgruppe Süd being divided and re-titled as Heeresgruppe A under Generalfeldmarschall Wilhelm List and

Alexander found the site of the pontoon bridge near the village of Berezovskiy, five kilometres north of Kalach.
(Alexander Trofimov)

Heeresgruppe B under Generaloberst Maximilian Freiherr von Weichs. The two panzer armies (part of Heeresgruppe A) would strike out for Stalingrad, the 4. Panzer-Armee hugging the bend in the upper Don and the 1. Panzer-Armee the lower one, while the 6. Armee (part of Heeresgruppe B) would be left to manage the prisoners captured during the second stage of the offensive. This third phase would also see the introduction of two more German armies, Generaloberst Richard Ruoff's 17. Armee, and Generaloberst Erich von Manstein's 11. Armee, fresh in from the Crimean campaign, as well as the Italian Eighth Army under Generale di Armata Italo Gariboldi. These latter formations would also be incorporated into Heeresgruppe B with the

Meanwhile, the XXXXVIII. Panzer-Korps of the 4. Panzer-Armee, which had already crossed the Don much further downstream at the end of July, was coming up from the south-west, joining up with the right flank of the 6. Armee on September 3. Their lead units, the 14. and 24. Panzer-Divisions, occupied positions overlooking the southern half of Stalingrad. This machine-gun post, manned by troops of the 24. Panzer-Division, is positioned on what the Germans called the 'Kalkberge' (limestone mountains), a small rise overlooking the southern hillside suburb of Minina. When this picture was taken, on September 4, the high ground formed a small bulge in the front line and was under enemy fire from three directions. (BA Bild 101I-218-0517-15)

task of capturing Rostov, so opening the gateway to the Caucasus oilfields. By the end of 'Blau III', it was planned that a defensive line would have been established along the west bank of the Don from the Voronezh region (2. Armee) to the Stalingrad region (6. Armee) with various Axis armies in between. This would then cover Heeresgruppe A's plunge into the Caucasus and its intended capture of the oil cities of Maikop, Grozny and Baku (the still unwritten plan 'Blau IV').

With the meagre resources that the Germans had at their disposal, it was a truly ambitious undertaking to reach the gates of Stalingrad and the oil capital of Baku before the onset of winter. Ironically, while the Germans had been underestimating Soviet strength in early 1942, had been overestimating that of the Germans. However, the realities were dire. Germany had already burned through her precious oil reserves during the earlier campaign in 1941 and did not have nearly enough for a full-front offensive in 1942 – the whole reason for Operation 'Blau' in the first place. Indeed, Hitler even conceded that if he did not acquire the Caucasus oilfields in 1942, he would have to end the war.

Likewise, after 1941 the German Army was drained of both personnel and equipment which had forced the abandonment of a full-scale offensive in 1942. While better-quality equipment was on its way, many veterans of the Polish and French campaigns were now incapacitated or dead, being replaced with green replacements. One of the reasons 'Blau' had to take place in stages was

A 7.62cm Marder III self-propelled gun belonging to the 3. Kompanie of Panzerjäger-Abteilung 670 rolls up the slope of the Kalkberge to take up firing position near the complex of buildings known as the Leather Factory. Panzerjäger-Abteilung 670, an army troop unit, had two companies of Marders, each with six vehicles, and one company equipped with the lighter-armed 4.7cm Panzerjäger I Ausf. B. In the two weeks that the unit was attached to the 24. Panzer-Division (September 3-14), it knocked out a total of 32 Soviet tanks: 22 T-34s, two KV-1s, three T-60s, two T-70s and two T-28s, plus one KV-1 damaged. (BA Bild 101I-218-0526-26)

Volgograd has grown considerably since the war and new houses now occupy the valley of the river Elshanka and much of the slope of the Kalkberge. Alex took his comparison near the Sadovaya Railway Station, looking south towards Minina on the far side of the valley. (Alexander Trofimov)

because Heeresgruppe Süd was still in the process of rebuilding its formations and not all would be ready by June 28. At the same time, Hitler felt that the delay in starting 'Blau II' would give the fresh replacements vital adjustment time to build confidence for the coming offensive. So in terms of personnel, quality had decreased in the Wehrmacht while it had risen in its opponent.

Equipment-wise, most of the panzers from 1941 had been destroyed and the entire inventory had to be built up from scratch. Granted these were higher-quality models, but the same was true for the Red Army and they were greatly out-producing the Germans. As regards the 75mm-calibre battle tank

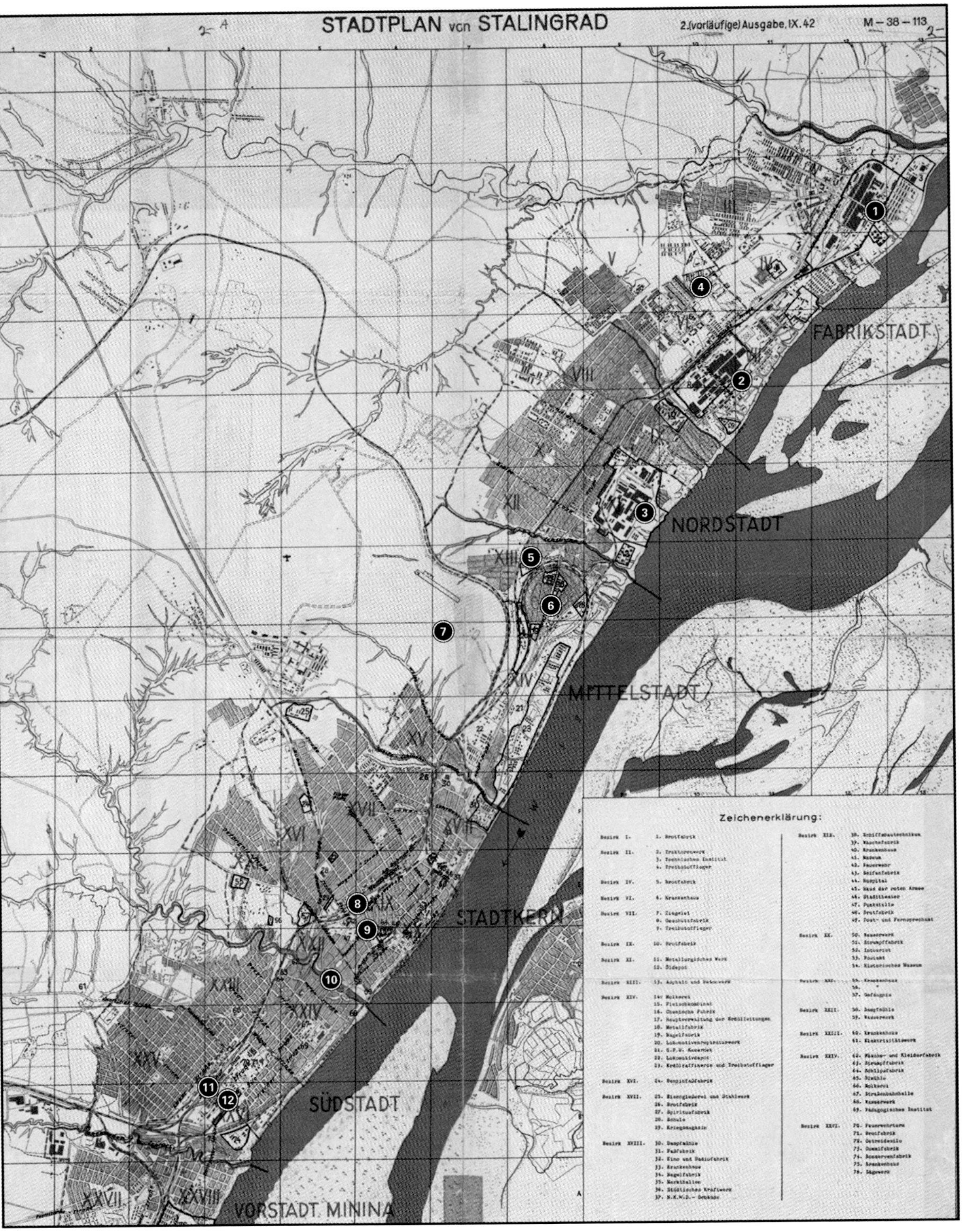

This city plan of Stalingrad was produced by the Reichsamt für Landesaufnahme (Reich Survey and Mapping Office), on the basis of aerial photographs in September 1942. We have indicated the main locations that featured in the battle. [1] Dzerzhinsky Tractor Factory. [2] Barrikady Gun Factory. [3] Red October Factory. [4] Schnellhefter Block. [5] Railway Loop ('The Tennis Racket'). [6] Lazur Chemical Plant. [7] Mamayev Kurgan (Hill 102). [8] Central Train Station. [9] Square of Fallen Heroes ('Red Square'). [10] Tsaritsa River. [11] Southern Train Station. [12] Grain Elevator. (USNA)

– the standard of the time – the Soviet Union was producing on average 1,265 T-34 and KV models per month, while the Germans were only achieving 73 new Panzer IV Ausf. F2(G). On June 28, Heeresgruppe Süd only possessed little more than a 100 and the other two German army groups combined had even less. If one adds in the excellent StuG III, the number of 75mm-calibre AFVs goes up to 124 per month for 1942, and if the Marders are included, one gets to 163 per month. The main battle tank for the Wehrmacht in Operation 'Blau' would have to be the obsolete Panzer III although at least by now it had been fitted with the more powerful 50L60 KwK 39 gun, 2,605 Panzer IIIs having been produced in 1942. As far as the Red Army was concerned, one must also not forget that for 1942 it produced nearly 5,000 45mm-gunned T-70s and received yet even more tanks via Lend-Lease.

Nevertheless, the victory fever which the campaigns of 1939-41 had infected the German leadership (and rank and file for that matter) was still very much alive in 1942 – it was almost as if the major setback at Moscow during the previous winter had just not happened. However, while Hitler was underestimating the Soviets, he was greatly overestimating the Western Allies, constantly fearing a landing that summer. The formations held in France included the 6., 7. and 10. Panzer-Divisions, the 1., 2. and 3. SS-Divisions as well as later expansion of the Infanterie-Division Grossdeutschland. Also, not only was Hitler returning panzer divisions to France from Russia to rebuild, he was also sending vital new war production there at the very time that it was desperately needed in the East.

To make matters worse for the Germans, on June 19 a German staff officer, Major Joachim Reichel, operations chief of the 23. Panzer-Division, crash-landed behind enemy lines carrying maps and notes on Operation 'Blau I', thus presenting Stalin with the entire plan for the upcoming offensive. While standard accounts tell us that Stalin dismissed this as enemy propaganda, and that he was still taken by surprise, there is reason to believe that this incident may have had a profound effect on Soviet decision-making in the early part of the offensive. Naturally the 'Reichel Affair' caused great consternation on the German side and in an attempt to minimise the damage, the code-names of the three phases of 'Blau' were changed to 'Braunschweig', 'Clausewitz' and 'Dampfjammer' respectively.

At the same time in Moscow, a radical change had taken place in the Soviet attitude towards their conduct in the face of future German offensives. Unfortunately for the German strategic planners, it took place at a time when Hitler had become the final arbiter in his army's affairs while Stalin was beginning to listen to his generals. Never again would he allow a catastrophic encirclement of his forces to the extent that the Soviet Union suffered multiple times in 1941 or, more recently in May, during South-Western Front's misfired counter-offensive at Kharkov. The Soviets were finally going to parry the Blitzkrieg and deny Hitler his massive encirclements he so needed to bring the Red Army to heel in 1942.

The all-out German assault on the city of Stalingrad proper began on September 13, the XXXXVIII. Panzer-Korps of the 4. Panzer-Armee attacking into the city's southern districts and the LI. Armee-Korps of the 6. Armee thrusting into the central district. For clarity's sake we will follow the battle from south to north, beginning with the attack by the 24. Panzer-Division into the portion of the city south of the Tsaritsa river. Following up on the initial attack by the 94. Infanterie-Division, this push began at 0300 hours on September 15. For this operation the division was divided into two combat groups. Gruppe Edelsheim, led by Oberst Maximilian von Edelsheim, the commander of Panzergrenadier-Regiment 26, was to make a swift thrust into the city and capture the city's southern railway station, while Gruppe Hellermann under Oberstleutnant Vollrath von Hellermann of Panzergrenadier-Regiment 21 would endeavour to secure positions to the east and north. Here tanks of Panzer-Regiment 24, part of Gruppe Edelsheim, turn left at the Voropovono-Stalingrad railway (which formed the boundary with the 94. Infanterie-Division to the south) to proceed eastwards into the city. The picture was taken by Kriegsberichter Geller of Panzer-Propaganda-Kompanie 694. (BA Bild 101I-218-0524-09)

The tanks started out from near the Leather Factory and with the railway line forming an easy reference point, Alex had no trouble in pinpointing the location. (Alexander Trofimov)

THE START OF THE OFFENSIVE (June 28-July 23)

Despite Germany's disadvantaged position in the war, on June 28, 1942 its Blitzkrieg machine functioned like old times. Hoth's 4. Panzer-Armee slashed its way towards the Don and Voronezh and encircled the Soviet 40th Army very early on. Although the advance was difficult in some places, for the most part Hoth was smoothly on his way to Voronezh over 150 kilometres away. Stalin was convinced that the Nazi goal for 1942 would be the conquest of Moscow, and had therefore placed his most-powerful reserves further back between the capital and Voronezh. As a result, the city fell on July 6 without a fight. This served Bock well because Hitler was adamant that Hoth must not get tied down in street-fighting. His instructions were, take it if it is easy, but do not lose any time over it.

The problem which arose however was in the grey area as both Bock and Hoth soon found themselves in an ever-increasing sea of red armour and extricating themselves was proving difficult. As German forces were approaching the city, Stalin had been directing tank units to converge on the area. This led in early July to one of the largest series of tank battles of all time, drawing in three panzer divisions (the 9., 11. and 24.) and three motorised infantry divisions (the 3., 16., and Grossdeutschland) against 11 Soviet tank corps (the 1st, 2nd, 4th, 7th, 11th, 13th, 16th, 17th, 18th, 24th and 25th) and several independent tank brigades in a two-week conflict covering over a 1,000 square kilometres.

With his 40th Army encircled midway between Kursk and Voronezh, and the Germans poised to capture the latter within days, Stalin ordered a counter-attack using his trump card: Major-General Alexander Liziukov's 5th Tank Army comprising over 600 tanks. Although with the advantage of air superiority the German attack brushed aside all the Soviet armour outside the city, on July 6 the 5th Tank Army was poised to strike from north-east of Voronezh into the German left flank. In addition, Stalin had placed the 3rd Tank Army behind the assault unit to be ready to exploit any successful breakthrough, and committed two additional tank corps, the 18th and 25th, close to the city itself. Thus, on top of the 800 or so Soviet tanks that they had battled over the past week, both Bock and Hoth unknowingly had another 1,000 tanks arrayed against them, set to strike the closer they drew to Voronezh.

In the event, the Soviet offensive was set off prematurely, and units were sent into battle independently, thus deprived of each other's mutual support. While the battle lasted for nine days, the Soviet counter-attack never placed German forces in serious jeopardy. Unbeknown to him, however, this futile attack launched by Stalin set into motion a chain of events that would radically alter German planning and set the stage for the dramatic showdown to come at Stalingrad.

Having reached the first houses of Stalingrad, the tanks of Panzer-Abteilung Lancken (Major Dietrich von der Lancken, commander of the III. Abteilung of Panzer-Regiment 24, exercised tactical command of all the regiment's panzers) wait while the infantry – the I. Bataillon of Panzergrenadier-Regiment 26 – clear the streets of the settlement. On the hill in the background is the suburb of Minina, objective of the neighbouring 94. Division. (BA Bild 101I-218-0528-10)

The same spot on what is today Morflotskaya Street, looking south to Minina. Alex pinpointed the location with the help of present-day inhabitants of the street who remembered the war from stories told by their parents. To gain the same height of the wartime photographer, he climbed onto a lorry. (Alexander Trofimov)

The Soviet Voronezh offensive effectively tied down Hoth's 9. and 11. Panzer-Divisions indefinitely, as well as the 3. Infanterie-Division (mot.) until the 14th, and while the Division Grossdeutschland and the 24. Panzer-Division were able to extricate themselves on the 9th, they were soon out of fuel. In the end, the Germans took 70,000 prisoners but the bulk of the Soviet units opposing the 6. Armee escaped to fight another day. Stalin did not wait for 'Blau II' to begin: as soon as the 4. Panzer-Armee began its assault on the 28th, he began to allow a flexible defence – or rather retreat – for the units on the Briansk and South-Western Fronts.

On July 13 von Bock was sacked by Hitler for having allowed his 4. Panzer-Armee to become mired in a tank battle north of Voronezh while he should have been proceeding south-east to cut off the Soviets confronting Paulus, although how 1,000 Red Army tanks were supposed to be contained without intervention from Hoth's panzers remains a mystery. Contrary to his rationale for having relieved von Bock, Hitler now allowed himself to sink ever deeper into delusion and convinced himself that the low bag of prisoners confirmed that the Soviets were on their last legs. When the armour from two of the three tank brigades from the 18th Tank Corps captured intact inside Voronezh was found to have been abandoned by their crews, the Germans saw it as a further indication that the Soviet field commands were having genuine trouble.

The Führer now inserted himself even more directly into the operations of his two southern army groups, and on the 16th relocated his headquarters from East Prussia to the Ukrainian city of Vinnitsa.

With von Bock's dismissal, Hitler continued to chase shadows by ordering the 4. Panzer-Armee to awkwardly cut across the line of 6. Armee's eastward

Looking west down Beloglinskaya Street in the Voroshilovkij district. Few of the wooden houses in the settlements that sprawled over this part of Stalingrad remain, most of them having been destroyed in the subsequent battle or been replaced by brick houses in post-war years. (Alexander Trofimov)

The grenadiers have completed their cleaning-out operations and the panzers move forward to join up with them. Most of the vehicles in this particular column belonged to the panzer regiment's 5. Kompanie under Oberleutnant Gert-Axel Weidemann. (BA Bild 101I-218-0528-13)

As Gruppe Edelsheim reaches the southern railway station around 1600 hours they pass close to what would become perhaps the most iconic building of the Battle of Stalingrad: the Grain Elevator, seen rising here in the background. It lay in the sector of the neighbouring 94. Division but they were held up and still a long way from it. However, realising its tactical importance, Gruppe Edelsheim sent a small force across the divisional boundary to take control of the building, which they found unoccupied. (NIOD 17274)

New warehouses and densely planted trees today make it impossible to take a comparison from the exact same spot where the photographer, Kriegsberichter Thiede, stood in 1942. This is the best match possible, taken from a point near the southern railway station. (Alexander Trofimov)

advance, to drive south and assist the 1. Panzer-Armee in creating a vast encirclement in the vicinity of Rostov – a move shrugged off as unnecessary by the latter army.

When this attempt also yielded a low count of prisoners, Hitler issued his Directive No. 45 of July 23, which replaced the original 'Blau III' concept in its entirety. Instead of the two panzer armies making a dash for the city on the Volga, they would now be diverted south across the lower Don and drive for the three oil cities. The new Operation 'Edelweiss' would now be the priority, and in its wake would follow three other armies: the 17. Armee, the Rumanian Third Army, and eventually Manstein's 11. Armee as soon as it arrived from the Crimea. Thus, a grand total of five armies under Heeresgruppe A were now set to initiate history's first mechanised oil war in earnest.

In contrast, the now supply-starved Heeresgruppe B received the secondary and less-interesting mission (Operation 'Fischreiher') of securing not only Stalingrad on the Volga but Astrakhan on the Caspian Sea as well. The strike force would consist of Paulus's 6. Armee and, as it advanced towards its objectives, it would drop off the Hungarian Second and Italian Eighth Armies as left-flank protection along the western bank of the Don, leaving the 2. Armee at Voronezh.

Hitler's offensive was now split and if one was to look for a specific moment when Germany sealed its fate in the East and, inevitably, in the entire war, a strong case would have to be made for the implementation of Directive No. 45 on July 23. In the act of sending both panzer armies south over the lower Don and into the Caucasus to chase the Soviets to the mountains near Grozny, the Germans lost critical supplies and, most important of all, irreplaceable time to neutralise Stalingrad, something that could have been achieved had the original tenets of 'Blau III' been adhered to in mid to late July. In the original planning of the summer campaign, the German leadership only regarded Stalingrad as an industrial and communications centre that had to be liquidated. It was not until the German forces began their drive into the Caucasus that Generaloberst Franz Halder, the Chief of the German General Staff, began to see Stalingrad as the key to the entire operation.

Stalin did not allow the Germans any room to compensate for their mistake. A week after the issuance of Directive No. 45, when Paulus and his 6. Armee had clashed into two new Soviet reserve armies and two new tank armies in the Great Bend of the Don, the entire German leadership including Hitler suddenly realised the importance of Stalingrad, and the battle for that city was truly joined. No German presence in the Caucasus could ever be secure with Red Army formations standing before Stalingrad, and it was also realised that by taking the city, a Red Army presence in the Caucasus would be virtually untenable. Whoever controlled Stalingrad would eventually win the Caucasus but not holding the city would jeopardise all the German endeavours in the south.

Unlike the Germans, Stalin had played this game before in the Russian Civil War of 1917-22 in this very region and he knew that a large army before Stalingrad was like a dagger aiming at the jugular of the Caucasus, namely Rostov. Hitler and his generals would become painfully aware that they simply did not have the forces to aggressively advance in two diverging directions at the same time. Immediately after learning of the Red Army build-up in the Don Bend just west of Kalach, the 4. Panzer-Armee was instantly turned north-east towards Stalingrad in support of Paulus. Heeresgruppe B was given priority in supplies and air support and now it was Heeresgruppe A's turn to play a subsidiary role. The rapid advance to the oil cities had come to an embarrassing halt.

THE APPROACH TO STALINGRAD (July 24-September 2)

In mid-July the Red Army began its defensive plan for Stalingrad by creating a new Stalingrad Front, its command transferred from Marshal of the Soviet Union Semyon Timoshenko to Lieutenant-General Vasily Gordov on July 23. Stalin reinforced the theatre with three fresh reserve armies (the 63rd, 62nd, 64th), the latter two (commanded by Major-General Vladimir Kolpakchi and Lieutenant-General Vasily Chuikov, respectively) being placed on the west bank of the Don to block any direct German advance to the city. In addition, two new tank armies, the 1st and the 4th, were formed and headed for deployment in the Don Bend.

Stalingrad itself was prepared for battle by the evacuation of livestock and food supplies, and the construction of bunkers, trenches and gun emplacements. Two days after Directive No. 45 was issued, the 6. Armee was dead in its tracks for lack of supplies, and was to remain so until the end of the first week of August, but now it was up against the new Stalingrad Front. This comprised seven armies, three of them fresh reserve armies and two in the process of conversion to tank armies, as well as the 8th Air Army. Paulus's force of 290 panzers was thus facing over 1,200 Red Army tanks with more on the way.

However, German tenure of the huge silo was short-lived. Led by Senior-Lieutenant Polyakov, a group of 27 soldiers from the Soviet 10th Rifle Brigade attacked in the late afternoon and recaptured the building, eliminating the last German defenders, who had holed up on the second floor, early on the 16th. Shortly after, Infanterie-Regiment 267 of the 94. Division arrived in the area and launched an immediate attack in the hope of regaining the storage tower. However, every assault was driven off with heavy losses. Infanterie-Regiment 274 took over on the 17th, but with equally little success, so a decision was taken to pummel the building into submission with artillery and Stuka dive-bombers. Howitzers, 8.8cm flak guns (from Flak-Abteilung 602) and heavy mortars were hauled into the area and began an uninterrupted pounding of the structure. Here a 10.5cm l.F.H.18 from Artillerie-Regiment 194 has just fired off a round. In spite of the devastating fire unleashed against them, the Russian defenders cooped up inside the elevator (which also included remnants of the 35th Guards Rifle and 10th NKVD Divisions, reinforced during the night of September 16/17 by naval troops of the 92nd Rifle Brigade ferried across the river) stubbornly held on for four more days, resisting numerous assaults with tanks and flame-throwers, and it was not until the evening of September 21 that a surprise attack from the north-west by Infanterie-Regiment 274 managed to rush the building, forcing the survivors of the Soviet garrison to break out. The 29. Infanterie-Division (mot.), which by then held the southern half of the cordon around the structure, took 104 of them prisoner but several small groups of Russians managed to escape across the river. By midnight, the grain elevator was finally in German hands. (BA Bild 101I-218-0529-07)

Built in 1940 of reinforced concrete, measuring 90 metres in length, 50 metres wide and 35 metres high, the silo survived the five-month battle relatively intact. The damage to its base, concrete pillars and the many shell holes that punctured its walls were repaired after the war and the building continues to be utilised today for the storage of grain. (Alexander Trofimov)

It was in the area immediately west of the southern railway station that one of the best-known images to come out of Stalingrad was made. Taken by Kriegsberichter Geller, it shows two veteran NCOs, both armed with sub-machine guns, in a crater in what appears to be a front-line combat situation. German propaganda exploited this picture to the full, using it in numerous publications. (NIOD 17283)

The Stalingrad offensive got off to an inauspicious start as Paulus's army soon was struggling in front of stiffening resistance. The lead units encountered the main line of resistance of the Soviet 62nd and 64th Armies on July 23. Although seriously low on fuel and supplies, Paulus began to unseat Kolpakchi's right flank and push him towards the Don to reach the strategic bridge over the river at Kalach. Significant Soviet armoured forces were sent to the Kalach bridgehead to bolster the position and by the 24th plans had been formulated for a counter-attack by the 1st and 4th Tank Armies, which included the 133rd and 158th Heavy Tank Brigades. Between July 25 and 28, 550 Soviet tanks were committed in the offensive to relieve the 62nd Army, being hammered mercilessly by the Luftwaffe on the open steppe while Paulus tried to hold on to and even complete his encirclement of the 62nd Army.

One of the lesser known battles of the Eastern Front, the Battle of the Don Bend, which began on July 23 and lasted until the final Soviet pockets of resistance before Kalach were eliminated on August 11, featured many interesting strengths and weaknesses on both sides. The veteran and under-strength Germans were critically short of both fuel and ammunition and had to be supplied by air, while the Russians were vastly over-strength in armour but short on tactical experience on the battlefield. In addition, accounts of Red Army personnel abandoning equipment and fleeing battle, echoing similar stories from Voronezh, Rostov and the Caucasus, were reaching both the German and Soviet leadership. A better-supplied German or a more-

However, a sequence of photos taken by Geller's colleague PK Leutnant Heinrich Sautter, who was working alongside Geller together with a cine cameraman, reveals that what looks like a genuine combat situation was in reality a staged scene. The PK team met the panzergrenadiers from Gruppe Edelsheim as they were escorting Soviet POWs to the rear and asked them to pose for them in a large bomb crater, to which they gladly obliged. This shot by Sautter shows Geller in the foreground just before or after exposing the famous frame. Far less dramatic than the other photo, it reveals that the road ahead is empty. The fact that Sautter himself is standing out in the open is a clear indication of the lack of any danger from enemy fire. (BA Bild 101I-218-0525-27)

Alex found the spot on Vokzalnaya Street, today Militionera Bukhantseva Street. The tram lines have been repaired. The buildings shown left and right have gone but Alex confirmed the spot using wartime aerial photographs. (Alexander Trofimov)

experienced Russian would have brought the battle to an earlier conclusion but, as neither was the case, the combat dragged on until August 11.

On July 31, several days after the great Russian armoured counter-attack against the stalled 6. Armee, and having seen the serious resistance Paulus had run into at Kalach, Hitler revised Directive No. 45 and ordered the 4. Panzer-Armee to relocate to Heeresgruppe B and support Paulus's drive on the city from his southern flank.

As the pressure increased in the Don Bend, Stalin finally reacted regarding the discipline and motivation problems in the Red Army and on July 28 issued his Order No. 227, aptly titled 'Not A Step Back!'. From now on, each Front would receive up to three punishment battalions, court-martials of officers retreating would be immediately convened, and well-armed blocking detachments would be instituted to 'supervise' less-reliable units. Cowards or panic-mongers would be shot on the spot. At the same time, Kolpakchi was relieved of his command and Lieutenant-General Anton Lopatin assumed control of the very troubled 62nd Army.

Although by July 30 the Soviet counter-attack had run its course, the lack of provisions still prevented the 6. Armee from regaining the initiative. The battle of the Kalach bridgehead (and the vital bridge itself) began on the morning of August 7 with the XIV. and XXIV. Panzer-Korps slicing behind the Soviet defenders with their backs to the Don river. The panzers had made contact by late afternoon, and a mopping-up operation then began with the assistance of the LI. Armee-Korps resulting in a further 50,000 prisoners being captured. Lopatin's 62nd Army was sent reeling across the Don, trying to regain its balance to form another defensive line in front of the city. The loss of hundreds of tanks added to the huge number already lost since Kharkov in May, and by the time the 62nd Army took up its defensive positions in Stalingrad proper a month later, none of its original five rifle divisions and two tank brigades existed. The 6. Armee was equally weakened and the loss of the irreplaceable veteran infantry would be sorely missed a few weeks later inside the city limits.

While Lopatin had been decimated to his immediate north, Chuikov (now deputy to Major-General Mikhail Shumilov of the 64th Army) had been able to skilfully fight a series of delaying actions in the face of the supply-starved 4. Panzer-Armee. Initially occupying positions on the Chir river and lower Don Bend, he moved his 64th Army to new positions on the Myshkova river as the 62nd Army was overrun, and the XXXXVIII. Panzer-Korps (General der Panzertruppe Werner Kempf) of Hoth's 4. Armee appeared deep in his left flank at Abganerovo Station. It was now clear to the Soviet leadership that the German panzer army was going to advance up the Simovniki-Tinguta corridor (the same corridor that Manstein would later use in his attempt to rescue Paulus's force in late December) towards the city, but when the lead elements of Hoth's panzers reached Tinguta on August 5, they came up against a series of fortified hills. The 4. Panzer-Armee stalled at this point until a wide flanking manoeuvre was conducted to the east in conjunction with the 6. Armee forcing the Don to the north. This gained Hoth another 20 kilometres.

Meanwhile, Paulus had forced the Don to the north of Kalach at Vertyachiy and Peskovatka and sent his XIV. Panzer-Korps on a daring direct thrust to the Volga. Hoth on the other hand would now have to redeploy his mobile units from east of Tinguta to the west and strike north from Myshkova to encircle the remnants of the 62nd Army and Chuikov's 64th Army well outside of the city.

As they moved forward into the southern part of the city, the Germans encountered numerous Soviet tanks, hastily thrown into the battle in an attempt to stop the enemy advance. This T-34 was knocked out near Kazanskaya Church, a few blocks north-west of the southern railway station. At the start of the battle on September 13, the 62nd Army had some 105 tanks (78 T-34s, 17 KV-1s and ten T-70s) in Stalingrad: in the city south of the Tsaritsa were the 26th and 133rd Tank Brigades with 35 tanks (the 26th had 18 T-34s and the 133rd 17 KV-1s, so the tank seen here most likely belonged to the 26th). In the central district were the 6th and 6th Guards Tank Brigades with 37 tanks, and near the Red October Factory in the north were the 27th and 189th Tank Brigades with 33 tanks. However, many of these AFVs were immobile and could only be used as fixed firing points.

Before the war this area was named Vozrozhdeniya (Renaissance) Square but today it is Kuznetskaya Street. (Alexander Trofimov)

Like Hoth, Paulus began his advance on the morning of August 21. The 295. Infanterie-Division seized a 25-square-kilometre bridgehead across the Don at Vertyachiy, and within 24 hours the XIV. Panzer-Korps (General der Infanterie Gustav von Wietersheim) was rolling across two 20-ton bridges. At 0430 on Sunday, August 23, the 16. Panzer-Division (Generalleutnant Hans-Valentin Hube) set out for the northern city limits, some 60 kilometres distant, with the Luftwaffe mercilessly pounding all that stood in his

Kriegsberichter Heine pictured men from a machine gun company advancing along a dual tram-line. The broken ground is evidence of the massive tactical air and artillery support that accompanied the attack into the city. (NIOD 17327)

This photo has previously been identified as having been taken in the 71. Division sector further north but Alex has positively located it to the part of the city south of the Tsaritsa river. The troops were moving south along Vokzalnaya Street, today Militionera Bukhantseva Street – the same street as where the pictures on page 74-75 were taken. The present photo was taken just short of the intersection with Novouznenskaya Street, i.e. some 1,200 metres north of the other location, and west of the railway line. This means that these troops were most likely from the 24. Panzer-Division (the 94. Infanterie-Division was responsible for clearing everything east of the railway line). The second building from the right on the slope still exists today but unfortunately it is hidden by the new housing erected in the foreground. (Alexander Trofimov)

Just on the other side of the railway, at the intersection of Socialisticheskaya and Barrikadnaya Street, an 8.8cm gun has been set up, its barrel trained north to protect against armoured counter-attacks from that side. Barrikadnaya Street was in the sector to be cleaned by the 94. Infanterie-Division and led east towards the Volga. (ANP 1851452)

The building on the right, a fire-station, has survived all the subsequent fighting and all post-war redevelopments in the city centre. (Alexander Trofimov)

path. By late afternoon, the citizens themselves were finally involved in the battle as the first raid took place. Not since the Blitz two years earlier had the Luftwaffe unleashed such power against a civilian population. Over 1,600 sorties pounded the city to create panic and choke the roads to try to prevent supplies reaching the front. As successful as this raid was – only three aircraft were lost – the 6. Armee would soon pay dearly as they fought their way into this city of rubble.

By nightfall, Hube's 16. Panzer-Division had reached the Volga with the 3. and 60. Infanterie-Divisions (mot.) desperately trying to protect his narrow supply corridor to the Don crossings at Vertyachiy. Before midnight, Hube received a personal order from Hitler to hold the Volga bank under all circumstances. The three divisions of the XIV. Panzer-Korps soon found

Over the following days, the 24. Panzer-Division slowly fought its way northwards until they reached the gorge of the Tsaritsa, thus securing the southern part of the city. Here, machine-gun teams from Gruppe Hellermann march north towards the river. The central city lies beyond. The heavy smoke billowing from one of the burning oil tanks at the Dzerzhinsky Tractor Factory in northern Stalingrad firmly dates this picture to September 17. (Ullstein 61458)

Alex's comparison was taken looking north-east from an abandoned cemetery on a hill in the Dar-Gora district of Stalingrad. (Alexander Trofimov)

themselves as isolated islands in an ever-increasing bombardment from Soviet artillery and ground assaults on their flanks. That night another heavy raid was mounted against the city by the Luftwaffe.

While the Red Army was putting intense pressure on the northern corridor, the South-Eastern Front commander, Colonel-General Andrei Yeremenko, pressed into service over 100,000 civilians and deployed armoured trains on the city's periphery. The civilian reinforcements were used for the construction of strongpoints and fortifications, and even proved effective at blocking German attacks until regular troops arrived. Factory workers continued to join the defence lines and some took newly-built T-34s (often without paint or gunsights)

The attack by the LI. Armee-Korps into the central part of the city on September 13 fielded two divisions: the 71. Infanterie-Division on the right and the 295. Infanterie-Division on the left. The mission of the 71. Division was to advance directly through the central city, across the marshalling yards of the Central Train Station and on to the ferry docks on the Volga shore. Advancing on the division's right flank, Infanterie-Regiment 191 aimed for the station and the Square of Fallen Heroes beyond. As it moved down Kubanskaya Street, the regiment was held up by this underpass blown by the Soviet defenders to create an obstacle. (BA Bild 101I-218-0539-27)

This has previously been identified as being a tram-line bridge along Vokzalnaya Street south of the Tsaritsa, but it is actually the railway bridge on Kubanskaya Street, just south-west of the Central Train Station. (Alexander Trofimov)

directly from the Dzerzhinsky Tractor Works into action. After Yeremenko allowed the evacuation of 200,000 children and elderly to the safety of the east bank, the only local bridge over the Volga was demolished. There would be no retreat . . . the army would fight to the last in the city.

Over the next few days, Hube tried in vain to advance into northern Stalingrad, even as his northern and western flanks came under intensifying Soviet pressure. Meanwhile, his isolated panzer division bled to death, deprived of manpower, ammunition and fuel. By August 28 he had made preparation for an emergency and unauthorised withdrawal towards the Don but fortunately the timely arrival of a relief column from the 3. Infanterie-Division (mot.) (Generalmajor Helmuth Schlömer) made his retreat unnecessary – at least for

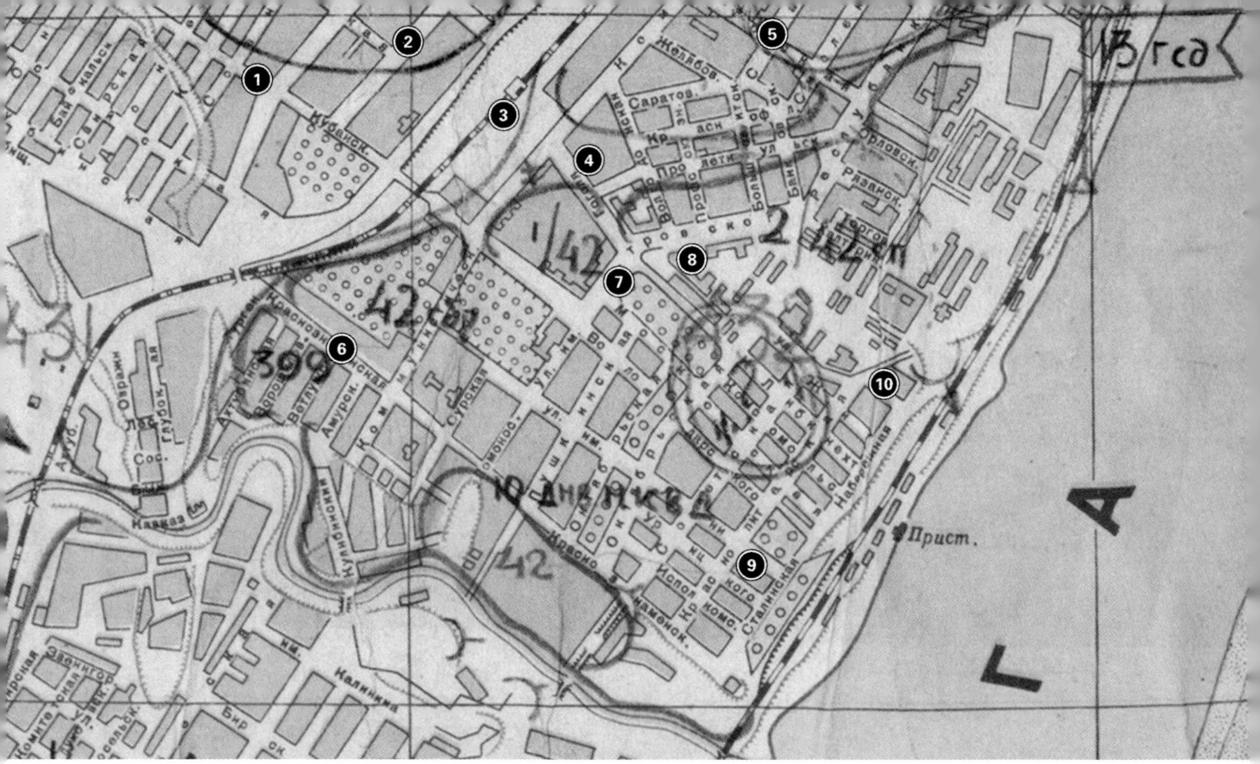

Stalingrad's central district. We have marked the streets and locations that feature in our photos. [1] Kubanskaya Street. [2] Parkhomenko Street. [3] Central Train Station. [4] Nail Factory. [5] Kurskaya Street. [6] Krasnoznamenskaya Street. [7] Square of Fallen Heroes. [8] Univermag Department Store. [9] Hulzonov Statue. [10] Palace of Physical Culture and Sport. (Library of Congress)

the time being. By late afternoon, a fierce Russian attack tore a five-kilometre gap between Hube and his westerly neighbour. Hube's corps commander, General von Wietersheim, then radioed Paulus that his position on the Volga was untenable and that he would have to pull back by nightfall but Paulus forbade the request. As Russian resistance closer to the Don was starting to whither, replenishment would soon be possible and the 60. Infanterie-Division (mot.) (Generalmajor Otto Kohlermann) was able to link up with the two isolated divisions of the panzer corps two days later.

On August 27, Stalin appointed General of the Army Georgi Zhukov as Deputy Supreme Commander of the Red Army (second in rank only to Stalin himself) and sent him to the besieged city two days later, just as Kempf's XXXXVIII. Panzer-Korps renewed its offensive from the south. Kempf made good progress, having bypassed the strongpoints around Beketovka to the east, and by the following morning he was only 40 kilometres south of the XIV. Panzer-Korps' Volga corridor. Von Weichs, the Heeresgruppe B commander, immediately sent instructions to Paulus to get his panzers moving south to complete the encirclement of Lopatin and Chuikov. However, although he was fearfully aware of the consequences, intense pressure on the Volga corridor's northern flank convinced Paulus not to gamble on sending his panzers to the south to link up with Kempf. By September 1 the window of opportunity had closed and Lopatin's 62nd Army had escaped into the city. The fight for Stalin's city would now be long and hard.

The battle for the Central Train Station began on September 14. The terminal building – seen here on fire in the background – changed hands several times but remained in Soviet possession after the 1st Battalion of the 42nd Guards Regiment of the 13th Guards Rifle Division recaptured it in a night counter-attack on the 15th. Over the next few days, bitter fighting took place in and around the building. The battle see-sawed across the big square in front, the Guardsmen finally being pushed back to a building known as the Nail Factory at the south-eastern end where they stubbornly held out despite being surrounded on three sides. The fountain that stood in the centre of the square, featuring a parapet mounting frogs and a group statue of six children dancing around a crocodile, became the quintessential image of this part of the battlefield. This picture, taken by photographer Emmanuil Evzerikhin of the TASS news agency, made the fountain the symbol of the devastated, yet undefeated city. (Novosti)

After the war the old railway station was pulled down and a new and much larger terminal, built in Stalinist architectural style, was completed just north of the old building in 1951-54. As part of this redevelopment, the fountain was removed and it was not until August 23, 2013 – the 71st anniversary of the start of the Stalingrad battle – that a replica was unveiled by Russian President Vladimir Putin. However, the new fountain was placed some 50 metres nearer to the station and built on a higher base. Also, on the new statue the figures of the children are not exactly the same as on the original, and the circle of dancers has been turned clockwise a little, hence a comparison that lines up the children not only shows the station very much closer, but at a different angle as well. (Alexander Trofimov)

THE GERMAN ATTACK INTO THE CITY (September 3-October 13)

By September 3, Paulus's and Hoth's armies had linked up and formed a united front less than eight kilometres west of the city. Stalin was meanwhile pushing Zhukov to launch a major counter-attack with the 1st Guards, 24th and 66th Armies against the German forces to the west of Rynok. Probably Stalin was not that optimistic over the outcome but he desperately wanted to divert German attention away from the city. On September 5 the attack commenced under Zhukov's personal supervision but with limited results.

Gunners from the 13. (schwere) Kompanie of Infanterie-Regiment 191 have set up their 15cm s.I.G. M33 artillery piece in a building on Kommunisticheskaya Street, on the southern side of Railway Station Square. The half-ruined building in the forefront, is the Kommunalschikov House (House of Experts of Municipal Services). The three-storied building seen on the far left is the Nail Factory (see the map on page 82). (SZ101394)

The same view today, looking south-east from Kommunisticheskaya Street into Gogol Street. The building that was the Nail Factory in 1942 today houses a telecommunications company.
(Alexander Trofimov)

Russian prisoners of war marching to the rear on Kommunisticheskaya Street in late September 1942, pictured by Kriegsberichter Herber. In all, the 71. Division took some 3,600 prisoners during its assault into the city. (NIOD 17284)

The same view looking south down Kommunisticheskaya. The apartment building in the background still stands. (Alexander Trofimov)

For the next week, Soviet ground attacks were launched by day while Soviet bombers raided German rear areas by night. Thus Zhukov bought precious time for Yeremenko to deploy his 62nd and 64th Armies in the trenches and fortifications on the outskirts of the city.

On the evening of September 12 Zhukov was back in Moscow conferring with Stalin and the Red Army Chief-of-Staff, Colonel-General Alexander Vasilevsky, on the dire situation confronting Yeremenko. During the meeting, the two generals had quietly discussed the prospect of finding 'another way out'. Stalin overheard this remark and demanded a plan by the following evening. The two generals spent all the next day devising a scheme to plough through the weak

As his troops approached the railway yards at a point north of the central railway station around noon on September 14, Oberstleutnant Fritz Roske, the commander of Infanterie-Regiment 194, spotted a number of Katyusha rocket-launchers (type BM-8-24 mounted on a T-40 light tank chassis) on Parkhomenko Street, just south-west of the station, firing to the west. He quickly called forward two 5cm PaK anti-tank guns and they in no time knocked out three of the so-called 'Stalin Organs' plus two Soviet tanks. The destroyed vehicles later got further chewed up in an artillery barrage, as evidenced by this picture taken a few weeks later. The building seen in the background was a vodka distillery. (Jason Mark)

Parkhomenko Street (see the map on page 82) was known as Donskaya Street until the 1930s but still appeared under its old name on some wartime maps. It runs one block west of the station, parallel with the railway lines. The old distillery, on the corner of Parkhomenko and Kubanskaya Streets, survives in mid-distance on the right-hand side. The view is looking south-west. (Alexander Trofimov)

Rumanian forces on Paulus's and Hoth's flanks to encircle the German forces fighting for Stalingrad. The seed for the Stalingrad pincer had been sown but it would be mid-November before the necessary reserve forces could be put in place.

On the German side, while Paulus was pre-occupied with stabilising his front west of Rynok, Hoth had driven a wedge between the 62nd and 64th

Once beyond the rail yards, the axis of the 71. Division attack was along two main streets leading down to the river, Kievskaya Street and Kurskaya Street. The infantry was supported by assault guns of Sturmgeschütz-Abteilung 244. Here a StuG III Ausf. B rolls along Smolenskaya Street, a side street of Kurskaya, loaded with troops from the I. Bataillon of Infanterie-Regiment 194, pictured by Kriegsberichter Heine on September 16. (NIOD 17270)

Today, Smolenskaya Street no longer exists, having disappeared with the redevelopment of the housing between Mira Street and Lenin Avenue. However, the house with the balcony seen on the left in the wartime picture survives, tucked away between the modern buildings so Alex had to take his comparison from closer in. (Alexander Trofimov)

armies, so isolating the former in the city. Just as the XXXXVIII. Panzer-Korps (14. and 24. Panzer-Divisions, 29. Infanterie-Division (mot.) and 94. Infanterie-Division) began its advance into the southern sector of the city on the 12th, Lopatin was replaced by Chuikov as commander of the 62nd Army.

It was on this day that Hitler summoned Paulus and von Weichs to the Wehrwolf FHQu at Vinnitsa. Despite the anxieties conveyed by his two generals, Hitler demanded a major assault on the city centre the very next day to augment the attack that was already underway in the southern suburbs. All objections raised by Weichs and Paulus – increasing Soviet

Here two of the StuGs (the one closest to the camera is the same vehicle as seen in the previous picture) roll eastwards down Kurskaya (see the map on page 82) escorted by infantry. At 1515 hours that afternoon, after overcoming several resistance nests and bypassing others, the force reached the banks of the Volga. (NIOD 17272)

Kurskaya Street has been renamed Port Saïd Street. After the war, new buildings were erected along most of its length.
(Alexander Trofimov)

reserves and attacks; exposed Rumanians on the flanks, and a withering 6. Armee – were swept aside by the Führer. The two men returned to the Volga that night to prepare for the following day. The attack was on.

At 0445 hours on the morning of the 13th, Paulus unleashed the assault elements of his LI. Armee-Korps (General der Artillerie Walther von Seydlitz-Kurzbach), in co-ordination with massed tactical air and artillery strikes on suspected Soviet strongpoints. The plan consisted of the 295. Infanterie-Division (Generalmajor Rolf Wuthmann) advancing eastwards to the Mamayev Kurgan (Hill 102) – the strategic hilltop overlooking the city – while the 71. Infanterie-Division (Generalmajor Alexander von Hartmann)

Shortly after Infanterie-Regiment 194 reached the banks of the Volga, Heine photographed a trio of soldiers from the I. Bataillon patrolling along Kurskaya Street. Considering that they are very close to the front line, the men look remarkably unconcerned. The building on the right housed the school of the KIM (Communist Youth International), the youth section of the Comintern, which existed from 1919 to 1943. (NIOD 17321)

The school block was later enlarged but the original building still stands: it is the part seen at the far end of the façade. Today it is no longer a Communist training institute but a secondary school named Lyceum No. 5 'Yuri Alekseyevich Gagarin'. It stands along the stretch of Port Saïd Street between the Central Train Station and the intersection with Mira Street. (Alexander Trofimov)

moved directly through the central city to the ferry docks. Each was to be supported by a StuG battalion. Units in the north were either considered too weak to join in the attack, or were already committed to defending furious Soviet counter-attacks in that area.

Chuikov's forces were in no better shape. While his 62nd Army was rich in divisions and tank brigades on paper, in reality the majority of these were mere shadows of their former selves. He entered the battle with 54,000 men and 105 tanks, his strongest unit being the 10th NKVD Division

A little further on, the patrol turned left off Kurskaya Street to walk across a large expanse of ruins. The buildings in the background were in the sector held by the regiment's III. Bataillon but they were unoccupied, the shortage of men forcing the Germans to only set up defences in buildings right on the forward line along the riverbank where they were under heavy counter-attacks from the Soviets. (NIOD 17298)

Now just a nondescript side street in central Volgograd. (Alexander Trofimov)

(Colonel Alexander Sarayev). This unit was flush with conscripted workers' militias and three of its five regiments were already spread out along the entire defence perimeter.

The German attack made good progress over the open ground west of the city, much of which was now in ruins, and there can be no doubt that every German soldier rapidly advancing toward the Volga just over three kilometres away now thought that this must be the end of the war. Communications to Chuikov's HQ on the Mamayev Kurgan had already been cut by the afternoon of the 13th, forcing him to relocate to the 'Tsaritsyn Bunker' just under a kilometre south of the Univermag department store. By noon on the 14th, the 71. Infanterie-Division had advanced to the Central Train Station from where the combat had to be fought building by building with vast amounts of rubble blocking streets to panzers and forcing them into Soviet kill zones. Chuikov's strategy was to abandon the traditional line of resistance

Having completed their sweep of the area the men return along Kurskaya in the direction of the railway yards. Although this well-known series of pictures show all the hallmarks of having been staged for the benefit of the photographer, the remarkable thing about them is that on the one hand they were taken so close to the front line, while on the other they clearly lack any sense of danger. (Jason Mark)

Amazingly, the three-storied housing block in the centre with the distinctive balconies still stands. This is one of just two original buildings which still survive along Kurskaya. (Alexander Trofimov)

and instead to fortify specific buildings to act as breakwaters against the German onslaught. Commanders were instructed to stay as close to the enemy as possible to help neutralise the Stuka attacks.

Casualties on both sides now rose rapidly as the battle descended into a bitter struggle for individual offices, staircases and cellars, and soon even the

Saratovskaya Street is today named Mira Street. On the far left is again the former KIM School, the only original building to survive around this intersection. (Alexander Trofimov)

A little to the rear, at the intersection of Kurskaya and Saratovskaya Streets, the crew of a 5cm PaK have set up their gun to guard against enemy counter-attacks from the side street. The piece was placed on the south-east corner of the crossroads and its barrel is pointing south-west into Saratovskaya. The shadow thrown by the gun shows that the photo was taken just after sunrise. However, the gun's parent unit is unsure: it could belong either to the 14. Kompanie of Infanterie-Regiment 194 (the regimental heavy weapons company) or to the 3. Kompanie of Panzerjäger-Abteilung 171 (the divisional anti-tank battalion). Note the abandoned Russian anti-tank gun across the street. (NIOD 17267)

sewers became battlegrounds as storm-troopers tried to outflank each other and emerge in the enemy's rear. Precision rifle fire and 88mm flak guns now gave way to the sub-machine gun, grenade, flame-thrower and spade. By nightfall on the 14th, the 71. Infanterie-Division had a narrow foothold on the Volga and was barely holding the now-exposed ferry sites under intense pressure from NKVD units. During the chaos, Germans advancing down the Tsaritsa Gorge even managed to bring Chuikov's bunker under direct fire, forcing him on the 14th to consider yet another relocation.

On von Hartmann's left flank, the 295. Infanterie-Division had overrun Stalingrad airfield and was engaged in a vicious battle for the Mamayev Kurgan hilltop against fanatical Soviet resistance from the 112th Rifle Division (Lieutenant-Colonel Vasily Sokolov) and 269th NKVD Regiment. All along the front, from the hilltop of the burial ground extending southwards to Minina, the city was engulfed in an incredible, intense inferno, a never-

This spot on Golubinskaya Street is one of the very rare locations in present-day Volgograd that has hardly changed since 1942. (Alexander Trofimov)

The battle in central Stalingrad continued unabated for almost two weeks as the Germans launched one attack after the other in an attempt to reach the banks of the Volga on a wide front. Throughout this period the infantry attacks were supported by assault guns of StuG-Abteilung 244. On September 24, two of its long-barrelled StuGs (commanded by Leutnant Ullrich Hempel and Oberwachtmeister Karl Pfreundtner respectively) were assigned to support Aufklärungs-Abteilung 171 (of the 71. Division) and the II. Bataillon of Infanterie-Regiment 276 (of the 94. Division) in a push along the Tsaritsa's north bank on the LI. Armee-Korps' right flank. Here Hempel's gun heads for the railway underpass south of the Central Train Station. (BA Bild 183-B22413)

The appearance of Krasnoznamenskaya Street today is a world apart from what it looked like in 1942, even the tram lines having changed. (Alexander Trofimov)

Having passed underneath the railway, the two StuGs faced Krasnoznamenskaya Street, a long straight avenue leading down to the river (see the map on page 82). Leutnant Hempel's gun, No. 202, has taken up a shielded position behind the building on the left. As he emerged from under the underpass, Pfreundtner (from whose vehicle this picture was taken) spotted a T-34 in the distance and immediately proceeded to knock it out. Smoke can be seen billowing up from the destroyed vehicle. (BA Bild 183-B22414)

ending cycle of German assault followed by Soviet counter-attack. With Chuikov's centre on the verge of collapse and the Luftwaffe sending in hundreds of sorties each day, he received support directly from Stalin. On the 13th, the Soviet dictator ordered the 13th Guards Rifle Division (Major-General Alexander Rodimtsev) to cross the river and the following day he

The tank knocked out by Pfreundtner was pictured by Kriegsberichter Herber some time later. The fact that the hatches are still closed is an indication that the crew was unable to escape and probably still lie dead inside the vehicle.
(BA Bild 183-B22359)

This is the same spot on Krasnoznamenskaya Street but not one of the wartime buildings has survived.
(Alexander Trofimov)

met with Chuikov to receive his orders: leave all heavy weapons on the east bank and bring 10,000 guardsmen over with only their personal weapons, anti-tank rifles and mortars, and clear out the central part of the city. With burning barges illuminating the river, the ex-paratroopers brought their first elements (the 1st Battalion of the 42nd Guards Rifle Regiment) ashore that evening while under fire from von Hartmann's infantry, just a 100 metres away. Immediately they charged the enemy positions and, together with the NKVD garrison, secured a bridgehead for the rest of the division to follow. At 2000 hours on the 14th, two regiments of the division (the 34th and 39th) began crossing and immediately set out to their objectives, stretched out from the city centre to the Mamayev Kurgan hilltop.

Battles raged throughout the night at strongpoints like the fortified House of Specialists, the Beer Factory, and the State Bank. Chuikov's plan was to commit one regiment each to the city centre and the Mamayev Kurgan

Another tank, this time a T-70, was knocked out at the eastern end of Lenin Street, just a few hundred metres short of the Volga. By the time Kriegsberichter Heine took this picture, in late September or early October, the Germans had erected a sheet-iron fence across the street in order to prevent Soviet observation from the east bank. (Ullstein 749063)

Earlier this photo was thought to have been taken on Theatre Square in southern Stalingrad but although none of the wartime buildings remain at this location, Alex is positive that it was taken here in Lenin Street in the central district. (Alexander Trofimov)

area, and to retain one battalion in reserve at his bunker on the Tsaritsa Gorge. However, on the following morning, the Germans began a new concentrated offensive in the south at Minina, as well as in the city centre which tied Rodimtsev's men down. His guardsmen, struggling to gain a foothold on the west bank, were being hammered relentlessly by dive-bombers, while the Central Train Station, which had been conquered and re-conquered more than ten times since noon the previous day, changed hands yet another four times during the 15th. By nightfall, the guardsmen had managed to push the Germans back 1,000 metres and had re-occupied Red Square and the train station.

Meanwhile, Chuikov had lost contact with the forces on Mamayev Kurgan and that evening he still had no idea who was in control of this strategic location. However, in addition to the successes in the centre, Rodimtsev's newly-arrived third regiment (the remainder of the 42nd) had now been

On September 27, the 71. Infanterie-Division finally secured the Volga bank along the entire divisional front and the 94. Infanterie-Division overcame the final resistance by the Soviet 42nd and 92nd Rifle Brigades around the mouth of the Tsaritsa, the last remnants of the latter escaping across the river. That same day, Kriegsberichter Pilz pictured men – either from Infanterie-Regiment 276 of the 94. Division or from Infanterie-Regiment 211 of the 71. Division – dug in on the river embankment, just north of the Tsaritsa river, in the shadow of the Monument to Victor Holzunov (1905-39), a famous dive-bomber pilot, squadron commander in the Spanish Civil War and Hero of the Soviet Union. Note the machine-gun team in the foreground who are armed with the brand new MG42 that had just been introduced. Its excellent reliability and high rate of fire would earn it the reputation of being the best machine gun to come out of the Second World War. (Jason Mark)

For some reason, the statue of Holzunov was turned 90 degrees after 1945. The avenue on which it stands was named Stalin Embankment during the war but has since been re-christened Embankment of the 62nd Army. This spot is just a little distance north of the riverside end of Krasnoznamenskaya Street (see the map on page 82). (Alexander Trofimov)

deployed to reinforce the river bank. A counter-attack was now mounted against the Germans on the hill using the remnants of the 112th Rifle Division, a battalion of the 13th Guards, and the 62nd Army's last ten KV-1 tanks of the 113th Heavy Tank Brigade.

Casualties in the city were staggering. The Germans had taken frightful losses in the past two days and the 13th Guards alone had lost 6,000 men. Entire units were being wiped from Chuikov's order of battle yet the fighting

raged on with ever-increasing intensity. Early on the morning of the 16th, Chuikov's counter-attack on the Mamayev Kurgan began and succeeded in relieving the beleaguered remnants of the NKVD on the east face of the hill and displacing the 295. Infanterie-Division from the hillcrest.

Seven kilometres to the south, battle groups from the 24. Panzer-Division (Generalmajor Arno von Lenski) and 94. Infanterie-Division (Generalleutnant Georg Pfeiffer) were involved in smashing Soviet resistance near the southern train station, while the 29. Infanterie-Division (mot.) (Generalmajor Max Fremerey) and 14. Panzer-Division (Generalmajor Ferdinand Heim) were clearing the Russians from the Leather Factory in Kuporosnoye. The defenders in the south were augmented by the presence of an armoured train yet by the 16th the Soviets had retreated to the Grain Elevator. This massive concrete structure dominated the whole of the city south of the Tsaritsa Gorge, and it quickly moved high on the German list of objectives as from this vantage point, accurate artillery fire could be brought down on every German unit operating to the east and south of Minina.

As the 24. Panzer-Division struck north through the railway yard to link up with von Hartmann, the 94. Infanterie-Division ran into increasing

Left: **Another 500 metres further north on Stalin Embankment, gunners have set up a 5cm PaK anti-tank gun in front of the Palace of Physical Culture and Sport. Its barrel is trained across the Volga.** (IWM HU5168)

Below: **This photo has previously been identified as having been taken at the Palace of Culture in Skulpturny Park in northern Stalingrad but this is not correct. The addition of columns with heavy stone plinths has considerably altered the appearance of the Sport Palace's façade but it is the same building. Today it functions as a musical theatre. The gun stood on the south-east corner.** (Alexander Trofimov)

The Univermag department store on the Square of Fallen Heroes (which the Germans referred to as Roter Platz – Red Square) was a key building throughout the battle. Fighting for the square broke out on September 15 as Infanterie-Regiment 194 (71. Division) grappled with tanks from the 6th Tank Brigade which Lieutenant-General Chuikov of the 62nd Army had hastily summoned from the southern suburbs on the 14th to block the German advance from the Central Train Station. Fighting around the square continued for several days. On September 21, the Germans renewed their assault, encircling the 1st Battalion of the 42nd Guards near the Univermag, where Senior-Lieutenant Fedoseyev, the battalion commander, had set up his command post. The following day they captured the building, annihilating Fedoseyev's CP and forcing the remnants of the battalion to withdraw further to the Volga. On September 26, after the last pockets of resistance in the city centre had finally been destroyed, Hauptmann Karl Fricke, commander of the I. Bataillon of Infanterie-Regiment 191, assisted by a few of his men, personally raised the Reichskriegsflagge over the entrance of the gutted building. It would remain flying there until the final German capitulation four months later. On January 26, 1943, faced with the inexorable shrinking of his encircled army's perimeter, General der Panzertruppe Friedrich Paulus, the commander of the 6. Armee, would set up his command post in the basement of this building. (BA Bild 183-B22531)

The Univermag was repaired after the war. However, today it is completely masked at the front by the large Intourist Hotel that was built on the north-east corner of the square, and can now only be seen from Ostrovsky Street which leads off beside the hotel. (Alexander Trofimov)

difficulties with Soviet troops in the Grain Elevator. Although by the 16th they were only 30 strong (the 35th Guards Rifle Division began the battle with 250 men), they were causing a real headache for the Germans. Following an urgent call for help, the 92nd Naval Rifle Brigade arrived that night and was immediately dispatched to Rodimtsev's left flank with a platoon being sent to reinforce the Grain Elevator.

For the next few days, the defenders in the huge silo stalled the 94. Infanterie-Division and thus left the right flank of the 24. Panzer-Division exposed to a counter-attack as it sliced its way north. After a German call to surrender was rejected, on the 18th the Germans

Hauptmann Fricke also authorised the establishment of a small cemetery on a strip of parkland just outside the Univermag. 'Here rest the fallen of I./I.R. 191. They died so that Germany will live', says the sign in this picture taken by Soviet war photographer Georgi Zelma after the German capitulation in February 1943. Between September 14 and 26 alone, the 71. Division had suffered a total of 208 men killed. (Georgi Zelma)

brought up 88mm flak guns and 105mm howitzers and began pulverising the structure. On the following day the Germans made ten assaults with infantry and tanks but all were to no avail. The Soviet resistance had held yet the defenders had taken losses. The grain had caught fire choking those inside; water both for the men as well as for cooling the machine guns had been depleted, and supplies of anti-tank rifle ammunition and grenades were nearly finished. Also, the only radio was out of action. After two more days of shelling, the Germans again went forward with 12 tanks and 200 assault troops. When the two Soviet Maxim machine guns were finally put out of action, the defence started to crumble. Although the Germans managed to enter part of the building, it was still difficult to locate and eliminate the defenders but that evening those remaining withdrew for lack of ammunition. Only a few men are known to have survived.

After the fall of the silo on the 21st, Soviet reinforcements poured into the

The same view today, looking east down Ostrovsky Street, with the Univermag on the right. What remains of the former House of Specialists is today the Hotel Old Stalingrad. (Alexander Trofimov)

On October 16, General Paulus carried out an inspection of the 71. Division which by then was responsible for holding the entire Volga frontage in central and southern Stalingrad. As part of his tour he visited a battalion command post in the Univermag which was then in the sector occupied by Infanterie-Regiment 194. Here he is seen in the street outside the building (L-R): Generalmajor Alexander von Hartmann, the commander of the 71. Division; an unidentified battalion commander (perhaps Hauptmann Fritz Dobberkau of the I. Bataillon of Infanterie-Regiment 194); General Paulus, and Oberst Johannes Schmidt, the commander of Infanterie-Regiment 191. The building seen in the background is one of the many so-called Houses of Specialists in the city, in this case the House of Employees of Cultural Events. (Jason Mark)

The cemetery plot is now occupied by a modern annex built against the side wall of the Univermag. Under the circumstances, this is the best match possible, looking west down Ostrovsky Street. (Alexander Trofimov)

city under the cover of darkness. By now the 92nd Naval Brigade had been cut off and lay isolated along with the 42nd Rifle Brigade and 270th NKVD Regiment with their backs to the Volga on a miniscule strip of land just south of the Tsaritsa. As the 29. Infanterie-Division (mot.) and 94. Infanterie-Division kept them penned in against the river, German air and artillery pounded the pocket mercilessly. Chuikov had relocated his command post on the 17th to a position 800 metres north of the landing stage at the Red October Factory and now had received additional reinforcements, namely the 95th Rifle Division (Colonel Vasily Gorishny); the 137th Tank Brigade with just over a dozen T-60 tanks; the 284th Siberian Rifle Division (Colonel Nikolai Batyuk), and the 193rd Rifle Division (Major-General Fedor Smekhotvorov).

Bordering on the eastern side of Square of Fallen Heroes was a large park, which during the battle became covered with trenches and dugouts. Bitter fighting took place all around the area – between Infanterie-Regiment 191 (71. Division) and the ever-dwindling Soviet defenders from the 272nd NKVD Regiment (10th NKVD Division) and 42nd Guards Rifle Regiment (13th Guards Rifle Division) – between September 14 and 27, an endless series of small-scale close-quarter attacks and counter-attacks, interspersed with Stuka dive-bombing. After the fighting had ceased, Kriegsberichter Bauer-Altvater pictured a fallen Soviet soldier near one of the underground shelters. The view is looking south, into Pushkin Street. (BA Bild 183-B22436)

Death no longer lurks among the trees. The entrance to ulitsa Pushkina is today spanned by an arch. (Alexander Trofimov)

These badly needed units were immediately rushed to the three active areas of the fighting: the Grain Elevator, the Central District, and the Mamayev Kurgan, the 95th Rifle Division successfully gaining control of the hilltop on September 19.

See-saw battles raged daily during this time for control of the train station, Red Square and the central docks, with one side gaining up to several hundred metres, only to lose it the following day. This continued until the 26th when Paulus, confident that the capture of the docks was within his grasp, took pressure off Rodimtsev and redeployed the 24. Panzer-Division to augment planned attacks on the Mamayev Kurgan and Red October Workers' Settlements.

The second phase of the battle began on September 27, when the 24. Panzer-Division plus the 389. Infanterie-Division (Generalleutnant Erwin Jaenecke) and the newly-arrived 100. Jäger-Division (Generalleutnant

Attacking on the left wing of the LI. Armee-Korps, the 295. Infanterie-Division began its assault on the northern parts of the central district on September 13. Its right-hand force, Infanterie-Regiment 518, made good progress and pushed into the city on the 14th, reaching the banks of the Volga at 1500 hours. That day, Generalmajor Rolf Wurthmann (left) met with Oberst Otto Korfes, the regimental commander (right), who was understandably elated about the achievement of his men. They are on Khoperskaya Street, about a kilometre west of the railway line. (Jason Mark)

This part of Stalingrad has changed so radically that Khoperskaya Street does not even exist anymore. The nine-storey apartment block that has replaced the ruined buildings is No. 8 Dvinskaya Street. (Alexander Trofimov)

Werner Sanne) began a strong attack towards the summit of Hill 102; towards the workers' settlements to the west of the factories, and shortly thereafter towards the Orlovka pocket in the north. With massed dive-bombers at his disposal, Paulus dealt a severe blow to the Soviet defenders in the target areas; so severe that Chuikov later admitted thinking: 'One more battle like that and we'll be in the Volga'. By evening, the Germans had taken the vital summit of Hill 102, and had the workers' settlements under intense pressure. Chuikov counter-attacked the summit with elements of the 95th and 284th Rifle Divisions supported by all the available assets the Red Air Force could muster. By the time the battle ended the top of the hill had been reduced to a no man's land, accessible only to the dead and dying.

On the 29th, battle was finally joined in the Orlovka salient, as Paulus threw parts of the 389. Infanterie-Division and 60. Infanterie-Division (mot.)

Protruding between the central and northern parts of the city, and overlooking the whole metropolis, was the Mamayev Kurgan heights (also known as Hill 102). A vital strategic position, it was clear to both sides that whoever held the summit would have control over the city. To defend it, the Soviets had built strong defensive lines on the slopes, composed of trenches, barbed wire and minefields. The first German unit to launch an attack on the hill was Infanterie-Regiment 516 of the 295. Division. On the morning of September 14, Kriegsberichter Herber pictured men of the regiment climbing the south-western slopes on their way to seize a large part of the hill. However, unknown to them, a battalion from the 42nd Guards Regiment of the 13th Guards Rifle Division was about to cross the Volga that same evening and, being rushed to the spot, would succeed in holding on to the northern slope. Thus began a bitter battle for possession of the hill which changed hands several times. (Ullstein 659480)

After the war the shape of the Mamayev Kurgan changed considerably after thousands of tons of rubble from the city was dumped on its summit, raising its height by some 16 metres and infilling many of the ravines on the slopes, including the Dolgiy Balka (Long Ravine) seen here. Despite the changes, Alex is still certain that his comparison is correct. He lined it up with Ternopolskaya Street, which is on the right in both pictures. The view is looking south. (Alexander Trofimov)

On September 16 two Soviet regiments stormed the Mamayev Kurgan and fought their way to the summit where bloody hand-to-hand fighting took place, with huge casualties on both sides. On September 27, the newly-arrived 100. Jäger-Division attacked and recaptured half of the hill but the Soviet defenders – the 95th and the 284th Rifle Divisions – managed to maintain their own positions on the northern and eastern slopes. After another day of costly but fruitless fighting the 100. Division handed the mission back to the 295. Division. The Soviet garrison held out on the key stronghold for four more months – until January 26, 1943 – when troops from the 21st Army relieved them. This picture, obviously a staged propaganda shot, was taken shortly afterwards. (Novosti)

Alex lined up his comparison by referring to the bend in the Volga. The view is looking east towards the Red October Factory. (Alexander Trofimov)

against the Russian forces there. To the south of Orlovka, the three German divisions in the vast wooded area to the west of the factories began a slow and systematic advance to the Red October and Barrikady plants.

While the German onslaught against Orlovka and the factories continued, Chuikov received additional reinforcements during the first four days of October. These comprised the 37th Guards Rifle Division (Major-General Viktor Zholudev); 39th Guards Rifle Division (Major-General Stepan Guriev), and the 308th (Siberian) Rifle Division (Colonel Leonti Gurtiev), supplemented by the light tanks of the 84th Tank Brigade (the heavier tanks being unable to cross the river due to loss of the larger ferries).

Except in the Orlovka salient, by October 6 the fighting had subsided as the German divisions gradually wore themselves out on the approaches to the factories that had been converted into formidable fortresses. Nevertheless, on the 7th, Paulus launched a powerful local attack which managed to gain 300 metres of ground towards the Tractor Factory.

GERMAN ATTACK ON THE FACTORIES (October 14-26)

A lull of several days now set in as the Germans prepared for a massive assault scheduled for the 14th. Chuikov used this precious breathing space to prepare his defences and launch limited spoiling attacks although these ultimately failed to draw the Germans out of their positions. On his right flank he placed the 124th, 149th and the severely weakened 115th Rifle Brigades, and the 282nd NKVD Regiment. This group was responsible for the Rynok-Spartanovka area. To their south, the Tractor Factory was defended by the 37th Guards Rifle Division that had recently arrived plus elements of the 84th Tank Brigade, 20 light T-70s having arrived on the evening of the 4th. The remainder of the tank brigade defended the Barrikady complex along with the reinforced 112th Rifle Division, the 308th which had just arrived, and remnants of the 95th Rifle Division. Chuikov deployed two of the fresh formations, the 39th Guards and 193rd Rifle Divisions, on the western approaches to the Red October factory, which had halted the German eastward drive in its tracks. Batyuk's battered 284th Rifle Division clung onto the eastern slopes of Hill 102, and Rodimtsev's surviving guardsmen retained control of their narrow strip of land extending into the northern part of Central District, yet what strength Chuikov had in manpower, he lacked in equipment.

By mid-October, the 62nd Army had approximately 40 tanks left, the majority being light T-70s. While he could expect little support from the air force for the coming enemy assault, he did have access to powerful artillery assets deployed on the east bank of the river as well as four regiments of tracked BM-8-24 Katyusha rocket-launchers within the city itself.

After having just barely escaped from the German's clutches at the

In late September the struggle for the city shifted north, the Germans now aiming to capture the three large factory complexes along the Volga shore and their associated workers' settlements. The new offensive began in earnest on October 14, with the massive attack by the three divisions of Gruppe Jaenecke (14. Panzer-Division and 305. and 389. Infanterie-Divisions) towards the northernmost of the three plants, the Dzerzhinsky Tractor Factory. That day, a PK photographer from Luftwaffe-Kriegsberichter-Kompanie (mot.) z.b.V., Sonderführer Josef Ollig, followed an assault group operating on the right flank of the attack. A mixed force, made up of men from reinforced Infanterie-Regiment 577 of the 305. Division and panzergrenadiers from the 14. Panzer-Division, they formed up in the VTUZ higher technical school, a complex of brick buildings a few hundred metres distant from the south-west corner of the Dzerzhinsky Factory, where they waited while artillery softened up the target. H-Hour – 0730 hours – is only minutes away. (BA Bild 101I-617-2517-13)

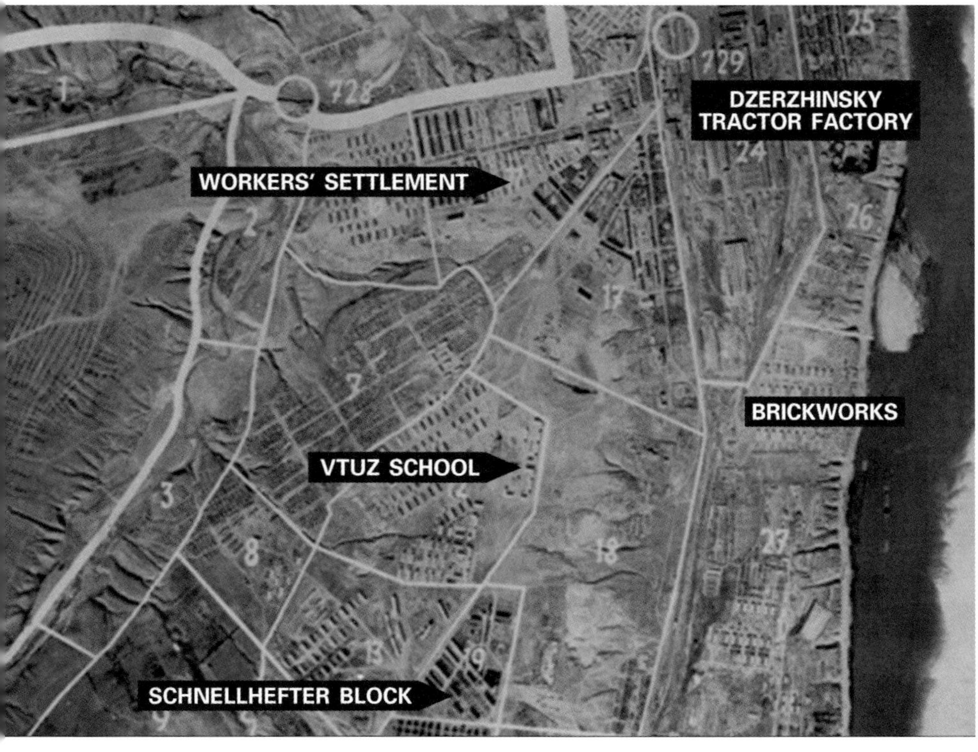

Between the VTUZ School and the group's objective – the brickworks south of the Tractor Factory – lay an open area covering several hundred metres. (USNA)

As they wait for the signal to attack, the men look up to Stukas diving down on enemy positions. These images, used in countless publications, have come to epitomise the German infantrymen in the battle of Stalingrad – combat-hardened veterans, laden with weapons and equipment, yet apprehensive at what is coming.
(BA Bild 101I-617-2571-15)

Amazingly, in spite of the destruction, the complex of buildings where these famous pictures were taken still survives. It consists of three blocks on Demyan Bedny Street. They all look alike but Alex is sure he has identified the correct one. This is the northernmost block, seen from the courtyard.
(Alexander Trofimov)

Tsaritsa, and having narrowly avoided incineration when the fuel tanks above his HQ were hit during a bombing attack, by October 5 German artillery had identified Chuikov's command post forcing him to relocate 450 metres to the north along the riverbank.

Meanwhile, even though his artillery ammunition stocks were dangerously low from the extended supply lines, Paulus planned to renew his attack on October 14, given the fact that he had just been granted the 14. Panzer-Division and 305. Infanterie-Division (Generalmajor Kurt Oppenländer) to spearhead the assault. Also the 79. Infanterie-Division (Generalmajor Richard Graf von Schwerin) was due to arrive any day.

Turning around, Ollig pictured the centre and southern blocks of the school. Smoke from an explosion – either from Soviet counter-fire or from a near-miss from the German preliminary bombardment – is drifting away. A Horch staff car stands parked next to the ruined centre block. The shot well illustrates that the VTUZ school lay completely exposed in a wide open expanse ploughed up by artillery. (BA Bild 101I-617-2571-17)

Today, the complex, now in use as a private school for infants, lies in a densely-built-up suburban area, and the view from the courtyard is further limited by trees that have matured. (Alexander Trofimov)

Paulus assembled the 14. Panzer-Division and the 305. and 389. Infanterie-Divisions into 'Gruppe Jaenecke' (named after General Jaenecke of the 389. Division) with the goal of capturing the Tractor Factory and then turning south to take the Barrikady Gun Factory. To their south, the 24. Panzer-Division and 100. Jäger-Division would launch limited attacks to the east in order to put pressure on Chuikov's front while the main attack flanked him from his right. In the north, the 94. Infanterie-Division and 16. Panzer-Division would march towards Spartanovka. The two remaining infantry divisions (the 71. and 295.) stationed in the central sector were deemed 'no longer capable of offensive actions' and would simply protect their areas from Rodimtsev's guardsmen and the threat of a Soviet amphibious landing to the south.

Directly in the path of the intended attack stood the Soviet 37th Guards and 95th Rifle Divisions, and the 117th Rifle Regiment (39th Rifle Division). The 112th Rifle Division covered their right flank, and the remnants of several infantry brigades were entrenched outside Spartanovka. Proceeding south from the 95th Rifle Division's positions were the 308th Rifle Division covering any direct eastward advance to the Barrikady complex, and the

As H-Hour approaches, the troops go forward to join up with their panzer support. On the right is the Horch car seen in the previous shot. (BA Bild 101I-617-7521-23)

The damage to the school building has been repaired. (Alexander Trofimov)

The men congregate at the end of the middle block. They will shortly move out into the open to advance across the open ground towards their objective, the brickworks to the south of the Dzerzhinsky Factory. (BA Bild 101I-617-7521-24)

The peaceful scene today belies the fact that this was once a hotly-contested and bloody battleground. (Alexander Trofimov)

193rd Rifle and 39th Guards Rifle Divisions further south guarding the Red October factory. The remainder of the defence line consisted of the 284th Rifle Division covering 'the Tennis Racket', so named after the peculiarly-shaped railway loop just south of the factories. Protecting the left flank were the remaining guardsmen of Rodimtsev's division.

The battle had been very severe and between September 13 and Paulus's mid-October offensive, his army had suffered nearly 20,000 casualties. In sharp contrast, Chuikov had taken approximately 60,000 casualties but had received over 50,000 reinforcements during the same period. Nevertheless, the morning of October 14 saw almost 100,000 men deployed against each other on an urban front bisecting Stalingrad for 12 kilometres. While Paulus was critically short of infantry, he still hoped it would be compensated by his advantage in tanks and airpower. If the fighting in Stalingrad had been considered 'savage' by this time, an attack of unprecedented ferocity was now about to unfold.

Meanwhile, a few hundred metres further north, Infanterie-Regiment 578 of the 305. Division, supported by an armoured combat group from the 14. Panzer-Division, was attacking the workers' settlement of the Dzerzhinsky Factory, prior to moving in on the plant itself. Here tanks and half-tracks of the Kampfgruppe (led by Major Bernard Sauvant, the commander of the I. Abteilung of Panzer-Regiment 36) have stopped on the western edge of the settlement, waiting for the infantry of Panzergrenadier-Regiment 103 to clear the multi-storied apartment buildings. (Jason Mark)

The street seen in the wartime photo was named Vtoraya Kolcevaya Street in 1942 but since the war the whole area has been re-developed creating new streets. This is now the intersection of Shurukhina Street and Street of the 95th Guards Division. (Alexander Trofimov)

Having relocated to a forward command and observation post in Gorodishche, six kilometres from the front lines, during the early morning hours of the 14th, Paulus was still able to witness the opening phase of the battle. Exactly at sunrise that October morning, the first of thousands of Luftwaffe tactical air support sorties struck the Tractor Factory with pinpoint precision. After the primary targets were hit from the air, German artillery began a continuous effort to suppress enemy positions as elements of seven divisions initiated their advance in light rain. By the following day Soviet forces had been squeezed into a small perimeter near Spartanovka, and by nightfall the Tractor Factory had been occupied.

By Chuikov's own admission, the 14th was the most critical day during the entire battle of Stalingrad. Once again he had to remove units from his order of battle and once again his headquarters ended up a couple of hundred metres from the front line.

The workers' settlement was fiercely defended by the 37th Guards Division and the panzergrenadiers needed seven hours of intense street-fighting from building to building before the armoured vehicles could pass through the rubble-filled streets. Note the transformer station on the right. (Jason Mark)

The housing blocks in this area all look alike and Alex spent an inordinate amount of time trying to identify the correct comparison. He settled on this one in Borby Street, one block south of Street of the 95th Guards Division, mainly because of the presence of a transformer-station (outside his picture to the right), as this is the only one in the entire neighbourhood, but he makes no claim that his comparison is 100 per cent certain. (Alexander Trofimov)

That evening Nikita Khrushchev, the political commissar of the Stalingrad Front, called Chuikov for a situation report. With the 37th Guards Rifle Division overrun, and the 112th Rifle Division and northern brigades cut off from the main bridgehead, he said that he had to concede the loss of the Tractor Factory if there was to be any hope of holding the remainder of the city. Help for the beleaguered defenders would have been useless anyway for communications had broken down so completely that Chuikov could only

While the main force moved on to the factory, other elements of Infanterie-Regiment 578 dug in on the edge of the settlement to hold the captured ground. In the lee of the building on the right stand two assault guns from StuG-Abteilung 245, which together with StuG-Abteilung 244 supported the 305. Division in this attack. (Jason Mark)

A fence prevented Alex from moving back further but this is the same block at No. 3 Shurukhina Street. The view is east. (Alexander Trofimov)

issue the order by runner: 'Fight with everything you've got, but stay put!' Even the unit guarding his own HQ was thrown into the fray when the 95th Rifle Division was outflanked leaving a gaping hole right next to his command post on the river bank behind the Barrikady. That evening, one regiment of the 138th Rifle Division (Colonel Ivan Lyudnikov) was ferried across and sent immediately into battle near the point of the breakthrough.

On the morning of the 16th, Gruppe Jaenecke turned south towards the Barrikady factory and had occupied half of it by noon despite the Soviets having been reinforced by the last two regiments of the 138th Rifle Division. By the time the factory had fallen on the 17th, the Germans were convinced that the city would now be taken within days. However, the substantial German advance had now brought them under the full weight of the Soviet artillery located on the east bank while fresh Soviet units continued to arrive on the western shore. Now the German units were pounded by heavy artillery of a calibre and concentration hitherto unseen from 152mm and larger siege artillery and repeated salvoes of Katyusha rockets.

He was dug in along Kultarmeyskaya Street, which since has been renamed Opolchenskaya Street. The building – named Stalin School No. 3 in 1942 – has been repaired and is still a secondary school today. (Alexander Trofimov)

At 1415 hours, the spearhead of the 14. Panzer-Division broke through the Soviet defence and, pushing ahead, penetrated into the grounds of the tractor factory near the main gate. By the end of the day, Infanterie-Regiment 578 had reached the western edge of the plant as well. Here a machine gunner from the regiment's III. Bataillon, in position just west of the main gate, faces south, ready for any enemy counter-attack. (Jason Mark)

The weather also turned against Paulus as heavy rain set in during the morning of the 18th, grounding his air support. The downpour, followed by snow, continued for two more days hampering the German efforts to mop up in the Barrikady factory complex. The skies cleared on the 21st and by the 23rd the ground was sufficiently hard for the 79. Infanterie-Division to begin its eastward advance on the Red October plant. This attack continued throughout the following day, as well as a renewed effort to eliminate the Spartanovka bridgehead to the north, but the troops of both the 14. Panzer-Division and the LI. Armee-Korps were exhausted.

Just a little to the south, and across the road from the factory, stood another secondary school, named after Sergo Ordzhonikidze, a veteran Bolsevik, member of the Politburo and close associate of Stalin, who had died in 1937. It too was heavily damaged in the fighting. (Jason Mark)

Today, it is known as School No. 12. (Alexander Trofimov)

This picture, taken by Kriegsberichter Bauer-Altvater, is almost always, but incorrectly, captioned as showing the main gate of the Dzerzhinsky Tractor Factory. In actual fact, it shows the terminal building of the Traktornaya Train Station, located along the same street but half a kilometre south of the actual main gate. The trenches and shelters in the foreground were constructed by the Russian defenders. (BA Bild 183-B22631)

Looking east from the park across the road from the station. The street running left to right on the western edge of the factory was named Ivanov Street in 1942 but is today Lenin Avenue. (Alexander Trofimov)

The real main gate looks similar but is decidedly more grand. (Alexander Trofimov)

From then until the end of October, the 79. Infanterie-Division struggled to mount attacks to capture even the smallest of buildings in the Red October factory area while being constantly being pounded by Soviet artillery. The German offensive had spent itself dry.

During the evening of the 26th, the lead battalions of yet another fresh Soviet formation – the 45th Rifle Division (Lieutenant-Colonel Vasily Sokolov) – crossed the river as the Front commander Yeremenko had personally promised Chuikov all the ammunition and replacements necessary to hold the remainder of the city.

Although the tractor plant went out of business in 2005, work is still carried out in some of the workshops. The area is off limits to the general public but, undeterred, Alex still ventured inside to match up Eckle's shot. (Alexander Trofimov)

The following day, October 15, the attack on the Dzerzhinsky Factory was resumed. Preceded by Stuka dive-bombing attacks, it began at 0700 with the troops advancing behind a rolling artillery barrage. While Infanterie-Regiment 578 was cleaning out the northern half of the plant, Panzergrenadier-Regiment 103 of the 14. Panzer-Division was doing the same in the southern half and by mid-morning the entire factory and the nearby Volga riverbank were in German hands. This unique photograph, taken by a soldier from Infanterie-Regiment 578, Hans Eckle, shows men from the 9. Kompanie of the IIII. Bataillon, led by Leutnant Klaus Voigt, inside the grounds of the factory. The regimental attack was supported by assault guns from StuG-Abteilung 245 and part of StuG-Abteilung 244, two of which can be seen moving up on the left. The view is west, looking back to the main gate. (AKG 74819)

A little further on, Eckle photographed what looks like the same two StuGs proceeding further into the factory grounds. The large building in the background housed the factory administration and offices. (AKG 74817)

The structure still stands but Alex found his comparison spoilt by trees, a low wall and new buildings. (Alexander Trofimov)

THE FINAL GERMAN ATTACK (November 11-18)

During this period of diminishing activity, Paulus was desperate for fresh forces to resume his attack. On November 1, he conferred with von Weichs and Generaloberst Wolfram Freiherr von Richthofen, the commander of Luftflotte 4, to discuss how the city could be secured before the weather took a dramatic turn for the worse, something that might be only days away. Having been caught unprepared in 1941, by the end of October winter clothing began to be issued to the 6. Armee yet poor weather would still cripple Paulus's already overtaxed supply route to the western railheads, and close air support would be practically neutralised.

While Richthofen offered Paulus a portion of the Luftwaffe's rail capacity in order to quickly stockpile the ammunition needed for the final attack, the 6. Armee's commander agonised as to how he could reorganise his line to provide von Seydlitz's LI. Armee-Korps with assault troops that simply did not exist. A request to the Oberkommando des Heeres (OKH – German Army High Command) for the bulk of the 29. Infanterie-Division (mot.) was rejected as the OKH would not sanction any further transfer of line divisions into the city. Instead, five assault engineer battalions were scavenged from army troops and various divisions outside the 6. Armee which reached Paulus between November 4-6. In addition, his two StuG battalions in the city would be reinforced with the first 12 units of a new 150mm infantry gun – the StuIG 33B – which was mounted on a heavily armoured PzKpfw III assault chassis. Together, this force was entrusted with delivering the final German victory that would eliminate the last Soviet bridgehead, and render the city secure before the onset of winter. Now Paulus, Seydlitz, and Oberst Herbert Selle, the Armee-Pionier-Führer (Commander of Engineer Troops) of the 6. Armee, began planning the final offensive to be named Operation 'Hubertus'.

After precious days of haggling between the German High Command and various generals concerning the offensive's participants, objectives and timing, a commander was nominated to lead the attack, scheduled to be launched on November 11. Major Josef Linden, himself a pioneer battalion commander and also director of the 6. Armee's specially created Pionier-Schule (assault engineers training school), began to take stock of his forces and set forth planning the offensive that was estimated to eliminate the last remaining Russian bridgeheads in the city. Across a battlefield littered with shell-holes, bombed buildings, rubble and twisted metal, the pioneers would systematically and methodically implement their craft at destroying one Soviet strongpoint after another. In their trail, an ad-hoc group of storm companies formed from all the remaining infantry and non-essential service personnel in the city, would provide cover and mop up after the engineers. Despite last-minute protests for proper infantry battalions from the 60. and 29. Infanterie-Divisions (mot.) to cover the pioneers, Seydlitz proceeded

The day after the fall of the tractor works, on October 16, the Germans pushed south along the Volga, launching attacks on the next industrial complex, the Barrikady Gun Factory. The force assembled for this assault comprised Infanterie-Regiment 577, elements of Panzergrenadier-Regiment 103, Kradschützen-Bataillon 64 and one tank battalion from Panzer-Regiment 36. Here foot soldiers of the 14. Panzer-Division – either from Panzergrenadier-Regiment 103 or from Kradschützen-Bataillon 64 – move into the attack from their assembly positions just north of the so-called Schnellhefter Block. The latter, an important tactical objective (see the map on page 64 and the aerial photo on page 108), had been taken by the 24. Panzer-Division on October 4. Its peculiar name derived from the German word for office folder and was coined following the block's appearance on the city plan. The Soviets called it the Hexagonal Quarter. (Ullstein 20568)

Amazingly after all this time, the same apartments still stand on Opolchenskaya Street. (Alexander Trofimov)

with the unenviable task of stitching together his unconventional infantry force by scavenging men from every type of unit in his corps.

The plan itself called for decoy attacks along the entire line, from the XIV. Panzer-Korps near Rynok to the old city defended by the 13th Guards Rifle Division. The main assault would come from seven assault engineer battalions – Pionier-Bataillone 45, 162, 294, 305, 336, 389 and Panzer-Pionier-Bataillon 50 – against the Soviet strongpoints in the vicinity of the Barrikady factory. They would be supported by infantry of the 305. and 389. Infanterie-Divisions, themselves augmented by battle groups from the two StuG battalions, and company-size contributions from the 14. and 24. Panzer-Divisions and the 44. Infanterie-Division (Generalmajor Heinrich Deboi).

The major objective of 'Hubertus' would be to seize the Volga shoreline immediately to the east of the Barrikady factory. A somewhat lesser, yet significant attack would also be launched in the vicinity of the Red October plant by the assault engineer unit – Pionier-Bataillon 179 – and troops of the 79. Infanterie-Division, although this was considered of secondary importance. In addition to the Croatian Legion (known to the Germans as verstärktes (kroatisches) Infanterie-Regiment 369), the 79. Division would also be augmented by forces from the 24. Panzer-Division: two panzergrenadier battalions, a motorcycle battalion and its armoured engineer battalion, Panzer-Pionier-Bataillon 40. It is no wonder then that 'Hubertus' would become known as the 'Battle of the Pioneers'.

Chuikov, now in his new command post beside the riverbank east of the Lazur Chemical Plant, also considered his situation. His depleted army was holding two bridgeheads but neither one was more than 800 metres deep. The northern pocket was deployed around Spartanovka and the southern one at 'Pavlov's House' with a thin strip along the riverbank all the way north to the Brickworks. Chuikov had successfully conducted several local counter-attacks, and had steadily taken in replacements for some of his losses which had injected a much-needed morale boost to his army. Correctly anticipating another enemy attack in early November, he had ordered a much-needed reorganisation and consolidation of the battered defenders, and his defence now stood as follows:

To the north (Rynok and Spartanovka area), Colonel Sergei Gorokhov commanded an isolated composite force of 1,000 men from the decimated remains of a few brigades and an NKVD regiment.

Of the main bridgehead ranging from the northern boundary of the Barrikady riverbank through the Red October and Lazur to Pavlov's House stood seven eroded divisions, a rifle brigade, and a rifle regiment. Furthest north was the 118th Rifle Regiment (the only surviving combat unit of the 37th Guards Rifle Division), which was now under the command of their southern neighbour, Colonel Ivan Lyudnikov and his 138th Rifle Division (also augmented with the survivors of the now defunct 308th Rifle Division and defending the Barrikady area). On their left flank were the reinforced 95th

Heavy close-quarter fighting raged in the factory grounds for two weeks but by the end of October the 305. Division had captured all of the Barrikady's massive assembly halls, the only obstacles between them and the Volga being a few battered houses and the remnants of the Soviet 138th Rifle Division. A final German attack on November 11, spearheaded by five fresh battalions of assault engineers, cut the Soviets off from the river, leaving them only a tiny bridgehead. Grim fighting raged around this small patch of land – known to the Soviets as the 'Island of Fire' – for three months, but the exhausted and starving defenders clung on until December 21 when the 62nd Army managed to join with them. Even then, fighting continued until the end of the battle. Sometime in November, Kriegsberichter Fritz Gehrmann pictured two soldiers of the 305. Division bringing up food and rations (plus a pair of boots!) to the most forward positions in the Barrikady. They are in the southern part of the factory grounds, walking north. The building on the left is Hall 2 and the one in the centre Hall 6c.
(BA Bild 146-2006-0106)

Most pictures taken in the Barrikady complex – be they from German or Soviet sources – show only a landscape of devastated buildings, twisted girders and shell-holes, which stand little chance of being matched up – quite apart from the fact that the plant is strictly off limits. Under the circumstances Alex did well to match up this picture. (Alexander Trofimov)

Rifle Division, 45th Rifle Division, 39th Guards Rifle Division (reinforced) and 92nd Rifle Brigade (reinforced) covering the area of the Red October through the Lazur Chemical Plant and Tennis Racket, the 284th Rifle Division on the base of the Mamayev Kurgan, and the 13th Guards Rifle Division occupying the northern part of the old city. In reserve, the 193rd Rifle Division was held back to defend the supply ferry.

At 0340 hours on the freezing morning of November 11, a heavy barrage announced the opening of the Germans' final assault. Not only was the main attack supported by artillery, but Paulus had every division along the entire front in the city, from north to south, initiate deception attacks to help pin down Soviet forces and prevent Chuikov from reinforcing the Barrikady area. This heavy barrage was quickly matched with Soviet counter-fire. In the face of this intense shelling, the infantry of both sides could only hug the earth as tightly as possible and stay motionless until the barrage had relented. Selle's assault engineers now began their methodical and slow advance against the Soviet defences, being supported at 0630 by a lightning Stuka attack on the Soviet forward artillery observation posts. One by one, Soviet strongpoints were reduced by small groups of German sub-machine gunners, flame-throwers and teams with satchel charges.

Chuikov immediately counter-attacked by thrusting Gorokhov's infantry towards the Tractor Factory, but by noon his Volga bridgehead was split again as the assault engineers reached to within 600 metres of the river just south of the Barrikady factory, cutting off Lyudnikov and his defenders in a pocket measuring just 400 by 700 metres.

By evening Lyudnikov was running low on supplies and ammunition and the Pharmacy had fallen, yet at the same time casualties for the Germans had been severe, both in the Barrikady area and Red October, the latter attack having been a complete failure. As predicted, the heavily-laden assault engineers were quick to run out of ammunition, and often found themselves unsupported by the ad-hoc infantry teams to their rear. They had taken 30 per cent casualties, and were still expected by high command to take the Martin Furnace Hall in coming days if the efforts of the 79. Infanterie-Division proved fruitless.

Now constantly under fire from Soviet artillery, the exhausted German attack was suspended on the 12th to be resumed the following day. A few more buildings, including the formidable 'Commissar's House' were taken, but the Germans had to rest yet again the following day, limiting themselves to clearing one house at a time. Generals in command of hundreds of thousands of men spread out over many square kilometres were now reduced to issuing orders to battalions and companies the size of platoons, directing which house to take that day. Seydlitz attacked again east of the Barrikady on the 15th but achieved only modest gains and failed to eliminate the Lyudnikov pocket.

A spoiling attack by Chuikov during the evening persuaded Seydlitz to suspend his offensive for the following day. During the 17th and 18th, the final

German assault in the city resulted in only modest gains in the Spartanovka area. By this time, further attacks against the factories had become an exercise in futility, and the window for victory had at last closed for Paulus. Now, Rumanian observation posts were sending through reports of masses of Soviet tanks warming up their engines behind the front line.

Left: **The Red October Steel Works, lying south of the Barrikady, was attacked on October 23 by the newly-inserted 79. Infanterie-Division. In two days of stiff fighting they captured a large part of the plant but were unable to conquer its south-eastern corner, the keystone of which was the formidable Martin Furnace Hall (Hall 4). Defending the factory, along with units of the 193rd Rifle Division, was the 39th Guards Rifle Division. They doggedly held on to the factory for four months, until the final German capitulation. Sometime during the battle, Soviet combat photographer Georgi Zelma took this well-known picture of men of the 39th Division, assembled on the nearby Volga bank, being awarded with the Banner of the Guards.** (Georgi Zelma)

Meanwhile, on both sides casualties were mounting at an alarming rate. A German field hospital had been set up in the Russian-Orthodox church in the village of Gorodishche, eight kilometres west of Stalingrad, and as the battle progressed a growing number of cemeteries sprang up around it. This picture was taken by Generalleutnant Erwin Jaenecke of the 389. Infanterie-Division in late October when he left the city to assume command of the IV. Armee-Korps further west. (BA-MA N761-108)

Since the war the riverbank bordering the Red October Plant has been completely transformed, some stretches having been given a concrete embankment while others have been covered with trees. Another section has been altered by the construction of a new hydro-electric power station. The shape of the river itself has also changed but this is the same spot today, looking north-east. (Alexander Trofimov)

Today the site of the wartime cemetery is occupied by a large shopping complex. Most westerners live with the notion that the Russians had no qualms about building over German graves but in fact in most cases the remains of German soldiers were exhumed in 1943-45 and transferred to mass graves. As Alex says, 'Certainly, it was done primitively, since the war was still on, but it was done'. (Alexander Trofimov)

Zelma also photographed the numerous shelters, dugouts and other installations constructed by the 62nd Army along the river front. (Georgi Zelma)

With all the changes along the Volga riverbank, one cannot be absolutely certain where the Soviet photographer stood but, assuming that it was near where his other picture was taken, this is the best comparison possible. (Alexander Trofimov)

THE SOVIET COUNTER-OFFENSIVE (November 19-22)

Precisely at 0730 hours on the morning of November 19, 3,500 guns and mortars began the Soviet counter-attack, 160 kilometres to Stalingrad's north. The Stavka goal with Operation 'Uranus' was to rupture the front line manned by the Rumanian Third Army on Paulus's left flank, and to make a mad dash for the vital German communication centre of Kalach as it was there that the 6. Armee relied on a single pontoon bridge for their supplies.

The bombardment lasted for 80 minutes before the shock elements of the South-Western Front (5th Tank, 1st Guards and 21st Armies) and Don Front (24th, 65th and 66th Armies) charged the numbed Rumanian defenders who by noon had been largely routed. At 1300 hours the tank elements of the 5th Tank Army and 21st Army delivered the coup de grâce against the Rumanians.

The first indication of the magnitude of the disaster facing the Germans was when a temporary break in the clouds allowed a Luftwaffe plane to spot the westward advance of hundreds of Soviet tanks. At 2200 hours, von Weichs sent a message to Paulus ordering him to suspend indefinitely all further attacks in the city, and instead to redeploy the 14., 16. and 24. Panzer-Divisions to his left flank to meet the Soviet assault.

As Paulus's mobile reserve was now heading north-west, the disaster was completed on the 20th when the Stalingrad Front (51st, 57th and 64th Armies) to his immediate south began its offensive against the Rumanian defenders of the 4. Panzer-Armee. Due to shortages of fuel, Paulus's three panzer divisions could offer limited resistance to the northern thrust. The only real obstacle to stand in the 5th Tank Army's way was the XXXXVIII. Panzer-Korps and the only mobile reserve worth mentioning in the south was the veteran 29. Infanterie-Division (mot.), which was still nearly at full strength.

The XXXXVIII. Panzer-Korps comprised the 22. Panzer-Division with 40 tanks, and the Rumanian 1st Armoured Division with 80 obsolete Skoda and Renault tanks and was now being led by Generalleutnant Ferdinand Heim. Having formerly been in charge of the 14. Panzer-Division, he had assumed command of the corps on November 1 but was now destined to become the scapegoat for the Stalingrad disaster. In a sea of hundreds of Soviet tanks, the panzer corps was directed and redirected in desperation from HQ while communications between the two divisions had broken down. The snow now falling, together with fog, worked well in the Soviets' favour as the Luftwaffe was grounded and the German High Command was prevented from getting a firm grasp of the situation as a whole. In ideal terrain, the vaunted 88mm flak gun was the prime tank killer in the German inventory, but this too was rendered impotent by the weather.

The frantic misdirection of the panzer corps continued throughout the

A large number of images that show the battle of Stalingrad from the Soviet side were in fact not taken during actual combat but acted out for the benefit of the cameramen in quiet areas far from the front line or re-staged after the end of the fighting. This still from Soviet newsreel footage ostensibly shows Russian soldiers advancing past a knocked-out Panzer IV. (Critical Past)

It was actually filmed at the Sudoverf plant in Arsenyev Street in the industrial suburb of Krasnoarmeysk, over 20 kilometres south of the main city and six kilometres from the nearest front line. The filming was carried out in mid-October and photos taken on the same occasion already appeared in the *Krasnaya Zvezda* newspaper on the 28th. The footage was first used in the Soviet documentary *Stalingrad*, released in 1943, and has become stock material included in countless film documentaries since then. The building on the right was the factory's fire-station. (Alexander Trofimov)

A scene in the same sequence shows a housing block being hit by heavy shell-fire and infantrymen rushing in for the assault. (Critical Past)

This too was filmed in Arsenyev Street in Krasnoarmeysk and Alex found the same apartment building to prove it. (Alexander Trofimov)

Another clip shows a machine-gun team firing at enemy positions near a high-rise building. (Critical Past)

This turns out to have been filmed in Barrikadnaya Street in southern Stalingrad, probably in early September. It shows the yard of the House of Specialists of the Hydrolytic Plant. The housing block in the background remains. (Alexander Trofimov)

On November 19, the Soviets began Operation 'Uranus', launching a giant pincer movement by two army groups from north-west and south of Stalingrad. Within four days, the pincers snapped shut near the village of Sovetskiy, 45 kilometres west of Stalingrad, thus trapping 22 divisions – some 275,000 men – of the 6. Armee and 4. Panzer-Armee in a giant pocket. Six weeks later, on January 10, 1943, the Soviets launched Operation 'Ring' with the intention of attacking into the pocket to split it apart and capture the two airfields left in German hands. Here troops of the 21st Army advance past a knocked-out Panzer III at the town of Karpovka. Located 35 kilometres west of the city, on the edge of the German defensive perimeter (see the map on page 57), it was taken on January 13. The sector was defended by the 3. Infanterie-Division (mot.), so the vehicle most probably belonged to its Panzer-Abteilung 103.

Most pictures taken on the endless steppe west of Stalingrad, where the Soviet offensive and great encirclement – and the subsequent starving and freezing to death of numerous doomed German divisions – took place, offer little scope for comparison photography, so we have concentrated our story on the pictures taken inside the city. However, Karpovka makes a good exception, so we include it to represent the many actions that were fought on the snowy plains. (Alexander Trofimov)

next day but it only resulted in eventual encirclement. Its remaining 50 tanks were then ordered to break out to the south-west which they managed to accomplish over the next few days. By now the Rumanian armoured division had been destroyed and the 22. Panzer-Division had suffered such losses that it eventually had to be disbanded. Generalleutnant Heim was subsequently returned to Germany where he was stripped of rank and jailed without trial in a pathetic attempt by Hitler to whitewash his responsibility for the disaster.

Early on the 20th, the 29. Infanterie-Division (mot.) – in particular its panzer battalion – began a counter-attack against the flank of the Soviet southern thrust with some success. The division was ideally placed to continue its advance into the Soviet mechanised elements, and if the southern thrust had been thwarted, a spanner would have been thrown into the machinery of the entire 'Uranus' offensive plan. This may have been the

On January 22, the forces of Don Front, pressing in from the south-west, broke through the outer ring of the German forces holding out in Stalingrad and marched east into the city. The 62nd Army, finally able to break out from its long-held toeholds along the Volga, joined the offensive and together they swiftly split the starving and dying German forces in several isolated, doomed enclaves. Finally victorious, the Soviet forces took possession of the city centre. Here T-34/76s roll westwards through Oktyabrskaya Street. They are nearing the intersection with Lenin Avenue.
(Volgograd State Panoramic Museum 4716)

Today the street is named Geroyev Avenue. All buildings seen in the wartime picture have been demolished, the area having since been totally re-developed. (Alexander Trofimov)

last real hope for 6. Armee's salvation but on the 21st the division was ordered to withdraw and take up defensive positions on 6. Armee's southern sector, thus allowing the Soviets to freely complete their encirclement which was achieved on November 22.

A Soviet offensive was not a surprise to the German High Command – indeed one had been expected – but the strength of this attack was grossly underestimated, and the confidence in their ability to contain a breakthrough was unrealistically high. The Germans were in a good position

A kilometre further north, what may very well be tanks from the same unit advance through a landscape of snow-clad ruins. They are coming from Saratovskaya Street and turning into Kurskaya. This is the same crossroads where we saw the German anti-tank gun set up the previous September (see page 92). The photograph was taken looking east up what is today Mira Street. (Novosti)

The brick building in the right background is Stalingrad's historic synagogue. Built in the early 20th century, it was shut as a place of religion during the Communist era and, having survived the battle relatively unscathed, it was used as a state utilities' office until the demise of the Soviet Union. Restored in 2005-7, it was re-inaugurated in November 2007 and today again serves the city's Jewish community. (Alexander Trofimov)

A score of Soviet tanks assembled beside the Central Train Station, photographed from the pedestrian overpass at the terminal's northern end. The structure in the immediate right foreground is the station's water tower. As a vital transportation hub, the rail yards had been a target of devastating Luftwaffe attacks the previous August. (Volgograd State Panoramic Museum 4670)

The water tower has gone but these are the northern platforms as seen from today's footbridge. (Alexander Trofimov)

to counter-attack yet their primary mobile reserve, the 22. Panzer-Division, had been rendered relatively useless chiefly from neglect by the OKH to allocate sufficient maintenance and fuel resources prior to the 19th. The next day, when an overly-cautious Soviet commander penetrated Paulus's southern flank, aggressive and opportunistic action by Generalmajor Hans-Georg Leyser, the commander of the 29. Infanterie-Division (mot.), could have made good ground towards halting the enemy thrust, but at that critical moment the German High Command lost their nerve and ordered the unit to go on the defensive.

THE END OF THE 6. ARMEE (November 23, 1942 – February 2, 1943)

With the 6. Armee encircled, Paulus and Heeresgruppe B commander von Weichs wasted no time in requesting permission for a possible break-out, but Hitler immediately forbade any such action. Over the next days, and clearly aware of the dire military situation in southern Russia, Hitler looked for any possible hope of saving the fruits of his 1942 campaign and retaining his hold on the now politically important Stalingrad and the economically vital Caucasus. What Hitler was looking for, Reichsmarschall Hermann Göring, the Commander-in-Chief of the Luftwaffe, provided in a guarantee to keep Paulus adequately supplied by air over the coming winter weeks

With all hope being lost, Generalfeldmarschall Paulus (he had been promoted by Hitler the day before) finally surrendered on January 31, 1943. Here he arrives at the command post of Lieutenant-General Mikhail Shumilov, the commander of the Soviet 64th Army, in the town of Beketovka, located ten kilometres south of the city along the Volga (see map on page 57). This is Kalanchevskaya Street. With Paulus are his Chief-of-Staff, Generalleutnant Arthur Schmidt, just visible behind him, and his Adjutant, Oberst Wilhelm Adam, wearing a fur hat.

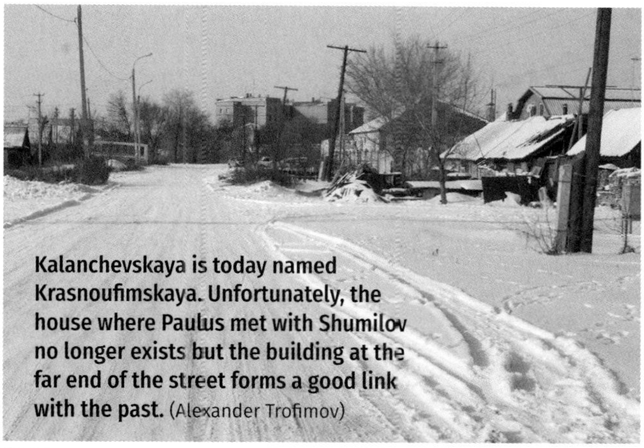

Kalanchevskaya is today named Krasnoufimskaya. Unfortunately, the house where Paulus met with Shumilov no longer exists but the building at the far end of the street forms a good link with the past. (Alexander Trofimov)

Soviet cameramen were present to film Paulus entering the house and, appearing to be ill at ease as he entered the crowded room, he sat down to face his victors. Although he surrendered personally, Paulus never formally surrendered his army.

and months until he could be relieved by ground forces. The Führer thereby made his final decision on the 24th for Paulus to hold fast and ready the 6. Armee for airborne resupply.

Soon after his decision, Hitler's resolve was strengthened when word came in from his chief strategist and newly-appointed leader of Heeresgruppe Don, Generalfeldmarschall von Manstein, that in his opinion a relief operation was preferred to a break-out, provided the necessary ground forces were made available. The battle of Stalingrad was

now transformed into a desperate war of manoeuvre as both sides raced to fill a gaping 200-kilometre hole in the Axis line between the Italian Eighth Army and the 16. Infanterie-Division (mot.) based at Elitsa. More men and material were quickly sent east in order to try to decide the outcome in 1942.

However, despite the valiant bravery and appalling losses suffered by the German resupply crews, Paulus never received what he had been promised, and Manstein's relief operation of December 12-23 failed in the face

Untouched by the war, the wooden house remains exactly the same. Alex even matched the snow! (Alexander Trofimov)

Some of the other German generals captured in Stalingrad were also taken to Beketovka. The officer on the left is Generalmajor Hans-Georg Leyser, commander of the 29. Infanterie-Division (mot.). He had taken over from Generalmajor Max Fremerey on September 25, when the division was withdrawn from the city for a three-week period of rest. Re-committed on October 19, it defended the south-western flank of the pocket, making a fighting withdrawal into the city until its last remnants capitulated on January 31.

The surrender ceremony over, Paulus was driven in his own staff car to Don Front headquarters outside Zavarykino, some 80 kilometres north of Stalingrad, to be questioned by General Konstantin Rokossovsky, the army group commander, and General Nikolai Voronov, the Stavka representative. Schmidt and Adam followed under escort in another car. The following day, February 1, the other captured Stalingrad generals were brought here too. Assembled in this picture are (L-R) Generalmajor Fritz Roske (71. Division), General der Artillerie Max Pfeffer (IV. Armee-Korps), Generalmajor Martin Lattmann (389. Division), Schmidt, Paulus, Generaloberst Walter Heitz (VIII. Armee-korps), Generalleutnant Alexander Edler von Daniels (376. Division) (with his back to the camera) and Generalleutnant Helmuth Schlömer (XIV. Panzer-Korps). All would face months of interrogation and years of imprisonment. (Volgograd State Panoramic Museum 2360)

After the war, as so often the case with small villages in Russia, Zavarykino had its name changed, to Zavarygin, but fortunately the house, outside which the German generals were photographed, still stands. (Alexander Trofimo)

of renewed Red Army vigour. In the end, the air and ground forces necessary to save Paulus never reached the front until the 6. Armee's airfields had been overrun and the pocket was on the verge of collapse. Potent German forces such as the SS-Panzer-Korps, Infanterie-Division Grossdeutschland and the Tiger tanks of schwere Panzer-Abteilung 503 arrived barely in time to stabilise the southern front and prevent a complete catastrophe that would have dwarfed the loss of the Stalingrad 'Kessel' (cauldron). Even a plan in January 1943 to buy Paulus time by crash-landing supply gliders, including the massive Me 321 Gigant type, was eventually scrubbed after the

After the German surrender, a large number of pictures were taken on the Square of Fallen Heroes. The Soviet army photographers realised that it offered a perfect backdrop to illustrate the German defeat and extol the Soviet victory. Many of their pictures, like this one, show groups of prisoners being escorted into captivity across the square. (Novosti)

The ruins along the northern side have since been replaced by the massive edifice of the Main Post Office. (Alexander Trofimov)

loss of Pitomnik airfield. Thereafter the pocket began its accelerating and unstoppable slide to its complete destruction.

True to Hitler's wishes, the 6. Armee never formally surrendered and was finally just overwhelmed and annihilated on February 2, 1943. Yet 11,000 men took refuge in the sewers and held out until early March when the last of them surrendered. While exact figures are not known, approximately a quarter of a million men were surrounded in late November, and while up to 40,000 were evacuated by air, around 100,000 were still taken prisoner when the end finally came. The healthiest were used to rebuild the city into what is today Volgograd but, of the others, a mere 5,000 survived captivity to be repatriated to East or West Germany in the 1950s.

Up to November 18, 1942, Paulus would have left an impressive military career for historians to study as he had been a gifted staff officer and competent field commander. Instead, he became the centre of controversy, largely due to his decisions regarding the Kessel. Having refused to

Waving the Flag of Victory over the embattled square! Several similar pictures, clearly staged for propaganda purposes, were taken from this same balcony belonging to the headquarters building of the Stalingrad Oblispolkom (Regional Executive Committee). It stood close to the square's southern end, on the corner of Lomonosov and Volodarski Streets. Visible on the far side (partly hidden by the flag) are the gutted remains of the Univermag – the site of Paulus's last command post. (Novosti)

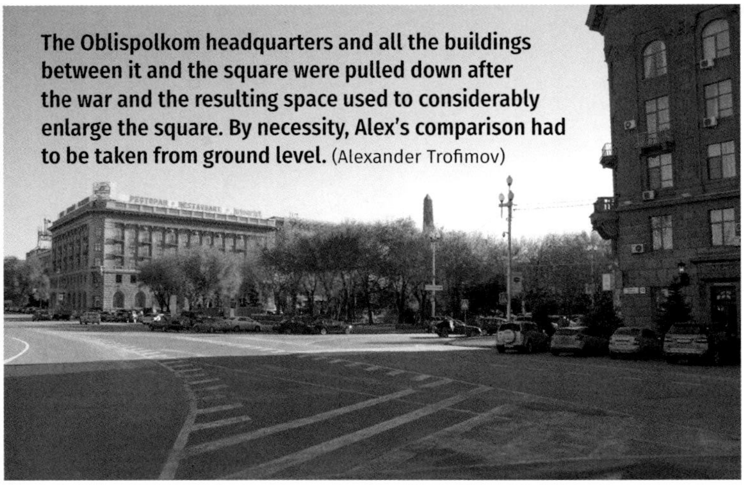

The Oblispolkom headquarters and all the buildings between it and the square were pulled down after the war and the resulting space used to considerably enlarge the square. By necessity, Alex's comparison had to be taken from ground level. (Alexander Trofimov)

disobey Hitler on several occasions regarding a break-out, and having refused to surrender the remaining pocket of resistance even after he became a prisoner on January 31, Paulus denied his Führer's last implied wish, which was for him to commit suicide. Hitler had promoted him to Generalfeldmarschall just in time to provide him with the incentive to pull the trigger, but Paulus chose life instead, and hence became the first German field-marshal ever to be taken captive.

On the other hand, General Chuikov's determined steadfastness in the Stalingrad bridgehead propelled him to a distinguished career. His 62nd Army was renamed the 8th Guards Army which, under his leadership,

Abandoned Wehrmacht vehicles fill up Lomonosov Street, the avenue that leads into Square of Fallen Heroes which lies in the background. Visible on the left is the rear side of the Drama Theatre, with the Oblispolkom building just beyond.

Lomonosov is today Mira Street. The building from which this shot was taken today houses the Volgograd Ministry of Health but, denied permission to photograph from one of its windows, Alex had to take his comparison from street level. (Alexander Trofimov)

Many of the German prisoners were put to work in the city clearing debris and obstacles. These men, clad in overcoats and scarfs against the freezing cold, are dismantling a road-block on Kubanskaya Street.

The ghosts of the past are long gone and trees have taken their place.
(Alexander Trofimov)

fought all the way to Berlin, and he had the honour of receiving the first peace overture made by the German Chief of the General Staff, General Hans Krebs.

In conclusion, the Battle of Stalingrad was essentially brought about by the failure of Operation 'Blau'. Due to poor planning and execution, the Soviet Army was not finished off in the summer of 1942, and while Hitler may have had delusions that the Red Army had already begun to collapse, the capture of Stalingrad was also endorsed by his generals as a way of making the Soviets stand, fight, and be destroyed.

Yet stand and fight they did, but by early October, with Paulus bogged down in Stalingrad, and Heeresgruppe A bogged down in the Caucasus short of the critical oilfields, Hitler became obsessed with the capture of the city in order to have at least a symbolic victory to show for the year's offensive campaign. Yet reality did not escape him that October. In the

Soviets rejoice in their victory over the Fascists. The two men in the foreground are dancing to the accompaniment of an accordion. (Novosti)

Looking north-west into Gogol Street. The Main Post Office stands on the right and the building with the tall spire seen rising in the background is the terminal of the new Central Train Station. (Alexander Trofimov)

The bulk of the 100,000 Germans captured inside the pocket were initially held in a number of POW camps located in Beketovka and Krasnoarmeysk, south of Stalingrad, which were collectively known as Camp No. 108. However, in the immediate aftermath of the battle, the Soviets found it impossible to provide food and warmth for such a large body of men and within two months over 50,000 had perished. Although conditions improved in the spring, by then it was too late. This gruesome picture was taken on the hillside outside Beketovka where the thousands of corpses were taken to be burned or buried in mass graves. (Novosti)

words of Generalleutnant Walter Warlimont, deputy chief of the OKW Operational Staff:

> 'Instead of greeting me when I entered the cabin, Hitler fixed me with a long malevolent stare and suddenly I thought: the man's confidence has gone; he has realised that his deadly game is moving to its appointed end, that Soviet Russia is not going to be overthrown at the second attempt and that now the war was on two fronts, which he has unleashed by his wanton arbitrary actions, will grind the Reich to powder.'

The spot where the wartime photo was taken is now a huge sand quarry, so Alex took his comparison 50 metres to the right, near the old Beketovka civilian cemetery, orientating himself by means of the group of large buildings on the left horizon and the power plant on the right. The quarrying removed all traces of the bodies buried here. However, there are similar mass burial sites elsewhere in the Stalingrad area and today the German War Graves Commission, in co-operation with local enthusiasts, are trying to trace these graves so that the remains can be disinterred and transferred to the German War Cemetery at Rossoshka, the new burial ground which has been established 35 kilometres north-west of Volgograd. It was opened in 1999 and now contains over 56,000 dead with commemorations to a further 120,000 who are missing.
(Alexander Trofimov)

STALINGRAD – THE FILM

By Karel Margry

IN 1993, 50 YEARS AFTER the event, the Germans at last ventured out to make a film about Stalingrad. Non-Germans usually do not realise the depth of the imprint which the defeat of Generalfeldmarschall Friedrich Paulus's 6. Armee in February 1943 made on German society. For the general public outside Germany, and for most military historians as well, Stalingrad is first and foremost one of the turning points of the war, an event of mainly strategic

The film. The attack on the Barrikady gun factory by Pionier-Bataillon 179 – on the left Feldwebel Pflüger (played by Mark Kuhn) with Hauptmann Musk (Karel Hermanek), with artificial right hand, the courageous and respected commander of the 2. Kompanie (Bavaria Film)

In December 1991, your Editor — on an altogether different assignment in Prague — happened to book into the Praga Hotel on Plzenska Street to find the hotel flooded with bloody-bandaged and grimy Wehrmacht and Soviet characters and most of the rooms stored with arms, uniforms and other props! It turned out that the hotel was around the corner from the deserted factory block which was being used for shooting *Stalingrad*. Although other duties precluded the taking of action stills, Karel did manage to get a few shots of the AFVs parked in the factory yard. (ATB)

and psychological importance. But for the Germans it is much more than that. It is a real national trauma and, for many Germans, still a taboo word, nodded at knowingly by those who lived through the war, but preferred not to be talked about in public. The trauma was caused, not so much because Stalingrad was, for most Germans, the first abode of an inevitable defeat, but even more so because of the sudden and permanent disappearance of over a quarter of a million men: of about 285,000 men surrounded at Stalingrad, some 146.000 died in the pocket; only 91,000 survived the inferno to become prisoners of war and, of these, a mere 6,000 ever returned home, the last as late as 1956. The bereaved families of those that did not return, especially in West Germany and Austria (for the Wehrmacht divisions at Stalingrad included about as many Austrians as Germans), and not forgetting the Rumanians and Italian troops caught with them, never knew whether they were killed in battle, succumbed to wounds, starved from hunger, froze to death or died in captivity. They just disappeared without a trace.

Ever since the war, the trauma of Stalingrad lingered below the surface of German and Austrian society. The sorrow and pain felt by the surviving veterans and the families of those that were lost was mainly channelled through the various veteran associations, the 'Traditionsverbände' and 'Kameradschaftsvereine'. These were usually divisional associations but, in the case of Stalingrad, the shared experience of that 'Kesselschlacht' (cauldron battle) and its aftermath was such that there were also formed in the late 1950s a 'Bund der deutschen Stalingrad-Kämpfer' (Association of German Stalingrad Fighters) in Germany and a 'Kameradschaft Stalingrad' (Stalingrad Comrades' Association) in Austria. Like most veteran associations

The screenplay begins in Italy in the late summer of 1942 in a sea-front Wehrmacht hospital. Unteroffizier Manfred 'Rollo' Rohleder (played by Jochen Nickel) and Obergefreiter Fritz Reiser (Dominique Horwitz), veterans of the fighting in North Africa with Pionier-Bataillon 336, are visiting wounded comrades and enjoying themselves with Italian girlfriends on the beach. The idyllic scene is interrupted by a battalion roll-call at which Major Koch, the CO, announces the news that the battalion is to form the nucleus of a new elite unit of sturmpioniere and introduces Leutnant Hans von Witzland (Thomas Kretschmann), a young and unblooded officer, as the new leader of the 1. Zug of the 2. Kompanie. Von Witzland's predecessor, Oberleutnant 'Lupo', seriously wounded, can be seen in a wheelchair in the top left corner, below the window. This scene was filmed on location in Italy in October 1991. (Bavaria Film)

of the Wehrmacht and Waffen-SS, they always kept a low profile, organising their own commemoration meetings and only seeking the limelight when advocating better financial and social security for its members. Compared to similar organisations in Britain or the United States, they shied away from too much publicity, certainly vis-a-vis foreign media.

Ever since the war, the Germans tried to come to terms with Stalingrad. It was a mental struggle in which sorrow and self-pity were besieged by guilt and reason. Because of the misery endured by them, both in the pocket and in the years of captivity, the common notion in Germany was to see the soldiers of Stalingrad as 'victims' and to describe the 6. Armee as 'the sacrificed army' – conveniently forgetting that Germany was the aggressor in the first place and that Russian prisoners of war fared even worse under German captivity.

As part of the coming to terms process, countless books were written

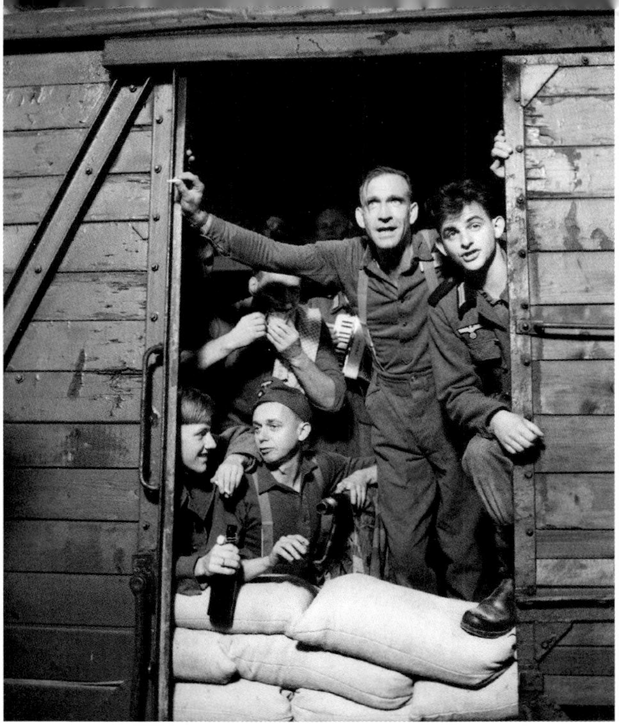

Two thousand kilometres further east, travelling in a troop train to the Eastern Front, the new lieutenant discloses to his men that their destination is Stalingrad. The troops are optimistic. Belief in German invincibility is still strong. At the Stalingrad reinforcement railhead, the platoon witnesses Russian prisoners being maltreated by German guards. Hans, the lieutenant, protests but is told to mind his own business by a callous superior, Hauptmann Haller (Dieter Okras). At a field service, held in one of the wadi-like depressions outside Stalingrad, the new men are welcomed by their company commander, Hauptmann Musk. Prominent in this still are Unteroffizier 'Rollo' Rohleder and Obergefreiter Fritz Reiser. (Bavaria Film)

Pionier-Bataillon 336, together with elements of Pionier-Bataillon 179, attacks the bitterly-contested Barrikady factory. Despite ferocious Russian resistance, they capture the factory, albeit with heavy losses. In the confusion of the fight, Sturmpionier 'GeGe' Müller (Sebastian Rudolf) (nicknamed so in order to distinguish him from the many other Müllers in the company) accidentally shoots his pal Dieter. Veterans Fritz and 'Rollo' try to console him. The men prepare the factory for defence. During a pause, they listen to a broadcast of Hitler's speech at the Bürgerbräukeller in Munich of November 8, 1942, in which he claims that Stalingrad 'has been taken'. Filmed at the old Poldi steelworks near Kladno, Czechoslovakia. (Bavaria Film)

That night, the lieutenant arranges a cease-fire with their Russian opponents to enable each side to bring in its wounded. The truce is broken by the fanatical Hauptgefreiter Müller ('Hundsgemeine' — the vicious dog), played by Oliver Broumis, who re-opens fire without orders. In the ensuing chaos, a Russian boy soldier, Kolja (Pavel Mang), falls into German hands. Still in the factory, the troops receive hot soup and mail. 'Rollo' learns that his wife is having an affair with a French POW. The demoralising news has hardly sunk in, when the Russians launch a surprise counter-attack. In danger of being cut off, the lieutenant, 'Rollo', Fritz, 'GeGe' and signalman Edgar (Heinz Emigholz) descend into the sewers of Stalingrad with a flame-thrower, hoping to find an escape route. The underground tunnels hide Russian soldiers, but also civilians seeking shelter from the fighting above. (Bavaria Film)

Separated in the dark from the other four, Hans bumps into a Russian female soldier, Irina, played by Dana Vavrova (in real life married to the director of *Stalingrad*, Joseph Vilsmaier). He promises to let her go if she shows him the way out but, before that happens, Irina escapes and Hans is re-united with his comrades. Shortly after, signalman Edgar is gravely wounded in a skirmish and has to have his foot crudely amputated with a knife. (Bavaria Film)

on the battle – by military historians, former generals, and novelists – and many documentaries on it were made. Yet, in all those years, there were surprisingly few feature films about Stalingrad in Germany. This in stark contrast to the Soviet Union where a score of films heralding the heroism of the Stalingrad defenders were produced – one of the most prominent being Yuri Ozerov's *Stalingrad*, released in 1989 and part of that director's multi-film project *Liberation*.

One of the very few German films about Stalingrad was *Hunde, wollt ihr ewig leben* (Dogs, do you want to live forever), produced in 1959 on a script based on the novel of the same title by Fritz Woss (Friedrich Weiss) and the book *Stalingrad – bis zur letzter Patrone* by Heinz Schröter. The latter had been a lieutenant in a Propaganda-Kompanie at Stalingrad and the one commissioned by Goebbels to write the Nazis' official 'heroes commemoration' book for Stalingrad. Although this was never published during the war, Schröter used it as the basis for his post-war book. Not surprisingly, the book, and thus the subsequent film, repeated the theme of the 'sacrificed army' and for that reason was acceptable for a German audience. That the subject was still highly sensitive was shown by another film, *Stalingrad*, produced by the West German broadcasting company NDR for television in 1963. Much more critical and openly questioning the personal guilt of the generals, it came under heavy criticism from Bundeswehr generals and stirred up a short but sharp public controversy.

For the next 30 years, whether the theme was too delicate, or because the marketing experts predicted that it could never be a box office success, or because the German film industry simply felt unable to recreate a historic battle of such importance and scale, no German film producer would take the risk of a film about Stalingrad.

The first treatment for another film named *Stalingrad* was written in 1982 by scriptwriter Johannes Heide. The rights to it were bought by the Munich-based film company Bavaria Film. Years went by, but nothing came of the project because Bavaria could not find a suitable partner for the project and, eventually, the company relinquished its interest.

It was picked up by Hanno Huth of Senator Film, another Munich film company, who, though aware of the unhealed mental scars over Stalingrad, was convinced that the German public was ready for a Stalingrad film and

The escape through the sewers. Note the use of captured Soviet sub-machine guns: 'They are reputed to be better than ours', one of the old hands says to a newcomer in an earlier scene. (Bavaria Film)

Finally, out of the tunnels, they manage to get Edgar to a first aid post. The boys are shocked by the misery and the sheer number of the wounded. Fritz forces a medic, whom he mistakenly takes for a doctor, to have a look at Edgar. Hauptmann Haller, who happens to witness the scene, threatens to have the group executed on the spot, but allows the lieutenant to plead his case at divisional headquarters. Director Vilsmaier used real war invalids and men with amputations for the horrific scenes in the first aid post. (Bavaria Film)

reckoned that, with the 50th anniversary of the battle coming up, a film on the subject could well prove a national and international success. Huth acquired the rights to the treatment, commissioned a first script to be written, and approached Joseph Vilsmaier to direct the film.

Vilsmaier, after a successful career as cameraman, with 28 films and TV productions to his credit, had turned to directing himself in 1988. His two films so far, *Herbstmilch* (1988) and *Rama Dama* (1990), had been widely acclaimed in Germany and won him several prizes. When first asked by Huth to direct *Stalingrad*, Vilsmaier refused 'because of the taboo surrounding the subject'. However, when, a few months later, first Günther Rohrbach, chief of Bavaria, and then Bob Arnold of ARRI (Arnold & Richter) showed an interest in taking part in the project, Vilsmaier shook off his doubts and accepted the job.

A producing consortium consisting of four partners – Royal Film (Huth),

Bavaria Film (Rohrbach), BA (Arnold) and Perathon (Vilsmaier's own film company) – was set up, with Vilsmaier as executive producer and Huth's Senator Film as distributing company. With a budget of DM 20,000,000 (approximately £9 million), it was one of the biggest German film productions of its time.

To orientate themselves on the subject, Vilsmaier and his co-producers first made a trip to Volgograd, the former Stalingrad. They toured the city and the battlefield, saw the various Russian memorials and visited the Museum-Panorama complex on the banks of the Volga (opened in 1985 to replace the old 'Defence of Stalingrad' museum). At the museum, they were shown letters of German soldiers – last letters which never reached their addressees, poignant testimonies of the suffering and desperation of the men trapped in the pocket. As Vilsmaier said: 'The letters had a strong influence on me. We were in this cellar of the Volgograd museum and suddenly we were shown these letters: December 1942, January 1943, that is shortly before the total collapse. One writer still did not believe that everything would go

In the divisional command bunker, Hans overhears General Hentz (a fictitious character played by Martin Benrath) explaining the 6. Armee's hopeless situation to his staff. The Russian pincers have closed behind the Germans and Hitler will not allow the 6. Armee to break out of the encirclement. (Benrath, seen here in the centre, as a teenager served as a Flakhelfer (Flak auxiliary) with an anti-aircraft unit during the war.) (Bavaria Film)

down; the other was already totally shaken up inside, realising full well that he would never get out. These letters are 50 years old. There were letters of hundreds of ordinary soldiers, bakers, cobblers, right up to officers. If one were to compare these with a hundred letters of today, one would see very quickly that no one can write letters like that anymore. People of often simple background were able in part to write almost philosophically. People today instead use the telephone. In any case, for me these letters were decisive, they erased the last doubts: this had to be filmed.'

Stalingrad was originally planned as an eight-hour television series, with a condensed version to be released as a cinema movie on the occasion of the 50th anniversary of the battle. However, since such a set-up meant that the television companies would have to wait some two years before they could screen the series and by then probably would have lost interest in it, it was decided to make only the cinema version. As a feature film follows different rules from a multi-part television series, the script had to be revised and

Hans and his men are not executed but sent to a penal company whose task it is to lift mines from under the snow. The weather is bitterly cold and the Germans lack winter clothing, supplies are growing thin. The troops are hungry and freezing. However, very soon, the men are recalled to the front. The situation is desperate and every man is needed. By now, discipline shows marked signs of disintegration but Hauptmann Musk, the company commander, manages to rally the men with a promise to rehabilitate them if they help to defend the Marinowka position, retaining which is vital for the envisaged link-up with the relieving Armeegruppe Hoth coming up from the south-west. Otto (Sylvester Groth), also in the penal company and an old friend of Musk, joins the group. Filmed on the polar plains of Kemijärvi, Finland, in March 1992. (Bavaria Film)

Director Joseph Vilsmaier (with beard) with his main actors. L-R: Thomas Kretschmann, Sebastian Rudolph, Sylvester Groth, Dominique Horwitz and Jochen Nickel. (Bavaria Film)

Vilsmaier took this opportunity to change certain aspects of the story. Arguing that 'with a historic catastrophe like Stalingrad it is difficult enough to show all the suffering that really occurred and there is no need for added Western-like elements', he took out some of the more Hollywood-style action cinema sequences. 'I was really concerned with reality', Vilsmaier said. 'I wanted to show, as far as this was at all possible, what it was like back then'. Vilsmaier made a thorough study of the historic events and consulted numerous military experts and participants of the battle from both German

Horwitz, Rudolph, Kretschmann and Nickel as they appear in the film. (Bavaria Film)

and Soviet sides. He then sat down and, together with Jürgen Büscher of Senator Film, rewrote the script.

From the beginning, it was clear to them that two approaches were out of the question: the story should not be told from 'high up' – no massive battle scenes alternating with scenes of generals at headquarters making momentous decisions; and it should not be a history lecture – no superimposed dates or arrows on a map to explain the development of the historic battle. Instead, they wanted to tell the story through the individual experiences of ordinary soldiers, of the men 'at the sharp end', with the generals appearing only on the side. Their story should be 'true', based on history and facts, but told through fictional characters. The screenplay should concentrate on a small group of men who find themselves thrown together in the giant meat-grinder that was Stalingrad. They share a series of experiences that can be said to be typical for the average soldier at Stalingrad. Each character should be seen as the symbolic representative of thousands of soldiers of the real battle. At the start of the battle they are all still victory-happy, still intoxicated by the success of earlier Blitzkrieg campaigns. As the tragedy unfolds step by step, each person reacts in a different way. However, none of the main characters escapes death. They all die. This was a deliberate choice of the scriptwriters. Vilsmaier: 'I know that when the audience watches a film like that and there is a survivor of the tragedy, the immediate feeling is: "perhaps I could be one of those survivors. And it wasn't that bad after all." So I said: whoever did not fall in battle in this tragedy, died of hunger or cold. There can be no heroes, no happy end.'

The script anchored its starting situation on a true episode of the historic battle. In early November 1942, in order to break the deadlock in the fight for the city, the German High Command despatched five battalions of Sturmpioniere, assault engineers specialised in street-fighting and working with flame-throwers, to Stalingrad, with special assignment to assault and force the capture of the hotly-contested factories in the northern part of the city: the Dzerzhinsky Tractor Works, the Barrikady Artillery Factory, and the Red October Steelworks. Arriving between November 4-6, the Sturmpioniere launched a concentrated attack on the Barrikady factory at 3.40 a.m. on November 11. Although they managed to push back the fiercely-defending Russians and gain a foothold in the factory, within 48 hours, their offensive had disintegrated into a series of isolated fights, not much different from the earlier fighting, and the new offensive had lost its impetus.

Lacking previous experience with war films, Vilsmaier chose his production staff very carefully. Several key men contracted by him for *Stalingrad* had worked together on a previous war film produced by Bavaria, Wolfgang Petersen's internationally-acclaimed U-boat film *Das Boot* (1982), notably the cutter, Hannes Nikel (who got an Oscar nomination for it in 1983); the sound editor, Milan Bor; and the special effects man, Karl Baumgartner. Especially Baumgartner, known affectionately throughout the film world as 'Charlie Boom Boom' was a veteran of many war movies, having previously

The use of severely disabled actors to re-create gruesome shots in the hospital and the attack on the factory sets the film apart from the Hollywood version of war. This short clip, where an unidentified German infantryman gets shot in half by a Russian tank shell at the battle of Marinowka is one which would cause British and American censors much concern. (All of this changed of course after Steven Spielberg released *Saving Private Ryan* in 1998.) However, it was only after we queried the name of the actor concerned with Senator Film that we realised it had been staged by digging in his legs, for this is none other than Oliver Broumis who plays the 'hundsgemeine' Müller. (Bavaria Film)

done the pyrotechnics for such classics as *Die Brücke* (The Bridge, 1959), *The Longest Day* (1962), *Weekend à Zuydcoote* (Dunkirk, 1964), *The Train* (1965), *The Blue Max* (1966), *Where Eagles Dare* (1969) and *Kelly's Heroes* (1970).

For the remaining crew, Vilsmaier chose people whose abilities he knew well, most of them having worked with him on either one or both of his previous films: music composer Norbert J. Schneider, art directors Wolfgang Hindhammer and Jindrich Goetz, make-up artists Ruth Philipp and Heiner Niehues and costume designer Ute Hofinger.

In all, the complete crew was to consist of 180 people from 12 different countries: Germany, Czechoslovakia, Russia, Finland, Italy, Switzerland, Austria, France, Holland, Belgium, Great Britain and the United States. For better communication, there were eight interpreters on the set.

For his cast, Vilsmaier contracted some 30 actors, most of them relatively young and new to the cinema audience. Before shooting started, the main actors went on a military training course, led by Captain Rick Squeri of the US Army, at the military training grounds at Hohenfels in Germany. The physical exercise and arms training not only heightened the authenticity of the later action scenes, but also prepared them for the rigours of filming on

On the icy, snow-covered plain of Marinowka, the men take cover in shallow trenches. The ground is too hard-frozen to dig deeper. They are inadequately armed and ammunition is scarce. Russian T-34s attack the position and threaten to overrun the thin line of infantrymen. In a pitched battle, the Germans sustain heavy losses but manage to knock out several tanks and fend off the armoured attack. Hauptmann Musk is wounded in action. This battle sequence was filmed partly in Finland and also at Kurivody-Hradcany in Czechoslovakia. The film company claims that their 13 Soviet T-34s dated from 1942, the armoured force being given more body by adding tanks supplied by the Finnish Army. (Bavaria Film)

location which, especially when the production was unexpectedly forced to move to within the polar circle, became unusually harsh. For his large set pieces, Vilsmaier mobilised no less than 12,000 extras (mostly Czechs) and, for his action scenes, some 60-100 stuntmen.

The Sturm Handels GmbH company supplied some 9,000 original Wehrmacht uniforms, complete with webbing, boots, fatigue caps, helmets, etcetera. Small arms, guns and grenades, all of World War 2 vintage and in perfect working order, came from the props department of the famed Barrandov Film Studios outside Prague.

As for AFVs, Vilsmaier's main prize were 13 Russian T-34s from Red Army depots in Czechoslovakia, all original 1942 models and in full working order, plus an additional ten Russian tanks, also of 1942 vintage, supplied by the Finnish Army. The tanks were transported to the various locations on low loaders, being driven during the filming by tank crews of the Czechoslovak Army. In addition to the tanks, Vilsmaier had half a dozen OT-810s, the Czech-built replica of the German SdKfz 251 half-track. From the Swiss company Ju Air came a piece of hardware vital to recreate the airlift out of encircled Stalingrad: one of the few surviving German Ju 52 transport planes. (Ju Air, based at Dübendorf near Zurich, owns three Ju 52s, all with original 1939 engines, which (until 2022) they used for pleasure flights, flying some 13,000 passengers annually.)

Wishing to ensure as much authenticity as possible, Vilsmaier secured the help of a team of technical and historical advisers: for the German side they were Generalmajor a.D. Jochen Löser, former Panzeroffizier Hans-Erdmann Schönbeck (retired president of the German Federal Automobile Industry Association but, in 1942-43, a young lieutenant at Stalingrad), and Hans Schwarzbraun (a former Sturmpionier and another veteran of Stalingrad); Professor Dr Daniel Projektor, retired colonel and long-time teacher at the Moscow Military Academy, was the Soviet adviser.

The next step was to find suitable locations. Although historical authenticity was one of Vilsmaier's top priorities, it was realised from the start that Stalingrad could not be filmed in the actual place where it had happened. Apart from the organisational and logistic difficulties of filming in the former Soviet Union, present-day Volgograd has grown and changed out of all recognition to what it looked like during the war, and Vilsmaier had to look for substitute locations elsewhere. After a long search, these were found in Czechoslovakia. With the fall of the Iron Curtain, eastern European countries had again become open to western film productions. Czechoslovakia had already enjoyed a short popularity with western film makers during the 'Prague Spring' of 1968, having for example provided the producers of *The Bridge at Remagen* with some very authentic-looking locations, and after the 'Velvet Revolution' of 1989 had again opened its doors widely to American and European film makers. To facilitate work in Czechoslovakia, Vilsmaier secured the co-operation of the film producing company Studio Sirotek, of the Ateliery Hostivar, and of the Barrandov Studios outside Prague.

Filming for *Stalingrad* started on October 22, 1991, in Italy, where the opening sequences of the military recovery hospital and the troop train leaving for Stalingrad were filmed. In November, the crew moved to Czechoslovakia for three months of filming in and around Prague. The producers had acquired the use of the closed-down Poldi steelworks near Kladno and of an old factory compound on the corner of Duskova and Plzenska Street in Prague-Smichov and these two locations were used for the scenes which were later combined into the episode of the German assault on and entrenchment in the Barrikady factory. The assault sequence alone, only eight minutes long in the final film, took three weeks to shoot, or, as actor Dominique Horwitz put it, 'three solid weeks of non-stop lying in muck'. At Smichov, much of the filming was done at night, both cast and crew enduring many uncomfortable hours in the freezing cold.

In January, the film team moved to Kurivody-Hradcany in Bohemia, formerly the largest Soviet training grounds in Czechoslovakia, but now vacated by the Red Army. Using the military airfield to stand in for the historic Pitomnik aerodrome, one of the four German-held airfields in the pocket, Vilsmaier here filmed the vivid scenes of the German wounded

Back in the relative shelter of ruined Stalingrad, the men are ordered to take part in the execution of Russian POWs. The pretext for the execution is 'sabotage' but the real reason is to save food for the besieged army. Among the prisoners lined up is young Kolja, the boy captured in the factory. Hans pleads to spare the boy's life but reels back at Hauptmann Haller's threatening question: 'Are you, a German officer, going to disobey an order?' Neither the lieutenant, nor any of his men, dares to refuse to pull the trigger. When one of Vilsmaier's German veteran advisers objected to the inclusion of this scene in the script, saying 'Things like that never happened,' the director checked with the Munich Institut für Zeitgeschichte. It transpired that in the last two months of the battle, there were no less than 348 public executions carried out by the 6. Armee. He left the sequence in — filmed at the factory location in Prague. (Bavaria Film)

and specialist troops waiting to be flown out of the encirclement and of the panic and chaos as the exhausted troops make a desperate run on the last Ju 52 taking off in swirling snow. Also at Kurivody, the art directors built a complete copy of one of those typical Russian steppe villages. Copied from pictures taken of actual villages in the Stalingrad area, it is seen in the film, almost in passing, being burned down by German troops.

Halfway through the shooting, an unwelcome accident completely bowled over the filming schedule. Driving his car on an ice-frozen road, director Vilsmaier slipped and overturned his vehicle, ending up in hospital with a broken hip bone. However, within six weeks he was back on the set, his body still in a corset and with a Munich specialist to look after him. (Vilsmaier promptly used him as a surgeon in the first aid post sequence.)

Nevertheless, despite the director's stamina, the delay caused by the accident threatened to have serious consequences. By the end of February, the snow in Czechoslovakia had almost melted away, but several of the snow scenes still remained to be shot. On short notice, a decision was therefore taken to move the whole production to Finland.

The transfer of the entire cast and crew with all its equipment and props to the Arctic circle, accomplished in a mere ten days, was in itself a logistical operation of some magnitude. The special problem of bringing the T-34s to the new location was solved by using a Red Army Antonov, the world's biggest transport plane, hired from Kiev, complete with its crew of 20 Russians, at the bargain price of DM 120,000 (£50,000). Four of the tanks were loaded into the plane at Prague airport, flown to Rovaniemi in Lapland and from there transported overland to Kemijärvi in the Arctic.

As far as is known, the tank battle filmed at Kurivody-Hradcany and Kemijärvi in sub-zero temperatures was, and still is, the largest ever shot for a German movie production. Although a relatively short episode in the

Back in their log dugout, the men's last shreds of morale have gone. Fritz is fed up with the war and wants to desert. Hans no longer feels himself bound by his oath to the Führer. Young 'GeGe' joins them. They are going to try to escape from the 'Kessel'. Only 'Rollo' stays behind, with Otto and the wounded Musk. In a snow-covered valley, the three weary deserters come across Russian civilians, sheltering in holes in the ground, starving and cold. In exchange for some bread, they point the way to the aerodrome. Further along, the three find heaps of frozen bodies of German casualties, left to die in the snow and with hospital tags still on them. They take the tags, hoping to smuggle themselves into one of the transport aircraft. (Bavaria Film)

For his film, Vilsmaier built a typical Russian hamlet, copied from pictures taken in the Stalingrad area, on the former Soviet training grounds at Kurivody-Hradcany. The airfield scene of the evacuation of the wounded was also recreated here. Note the five Czech OT-810 half-tracks. (Bavaria Film)

film, it is certainly one of the more realistic ever recreated on celluloid. It is one of the few which depicts the gruesome, but all too common technique of eliminating dug-in enemy infantry by having the tank dig its tracks into and on top of a one-man foxhole, burying and crushing the hopelessly-trapped soldier underneath. The audience is spared nothing: one German, running to attack a tank, is hit in mid-body by a tank shell at point-blank range and is seen screaming his dying breath with the lower half of his body lying beside him in the blood-coloured snow.

Shooting was completed on April 2, 1992. In all, some three tons of explosives and around 100,000 rounds of ammunition had been expended. No less than 87 people had been injured during the shooting period. Two persons sustained serious injuries: a stuntman and director Vilsmaier himself. In five months, the four cameras had exposed a total of 600,000 metres of film.

There followed nine months of editing, Vilsmaier and chief cutter Hannes Nikel and ten collaborators reducing the material to a film with a duration of 135 minutes. With *Stalingrad*, sound chief Milan Bor also introduced a technical innovation, it being the first European film production to mix its sound on the new digital (six-channel) Dolby Stereo SR*D system.

Before its release, the director and producers of *Stalingrad* were at great pains to explain that their film should be seen as an anti-war statement.

At the Pitomnik airfield, long lines of wounded and specialist troops wait to be flown out. Many soldiers have self-inflicted wounds and these are taken out of the line, dumped in the snow and shot. The examining doctor is fooled by the casualty tags of the three deserters. However, with one of the last Ju 52s preparing to leave, chaos breaks out as the desperate troops, oblivious of Feldgendarmerie firing into the crowd, storm the aircraft. None of the three manages to fight his way aboard and they have no choice but to return to their log bunker. The men have lost all hope. Their will to fight has gone. Waving his pistol, Hauptmann Haller tries to restore discipline. He shoots young 'GeGe', but is himself shot by Otto. Shooting their own superior officer is the group's only moment of triumph. (Bavaria Film)

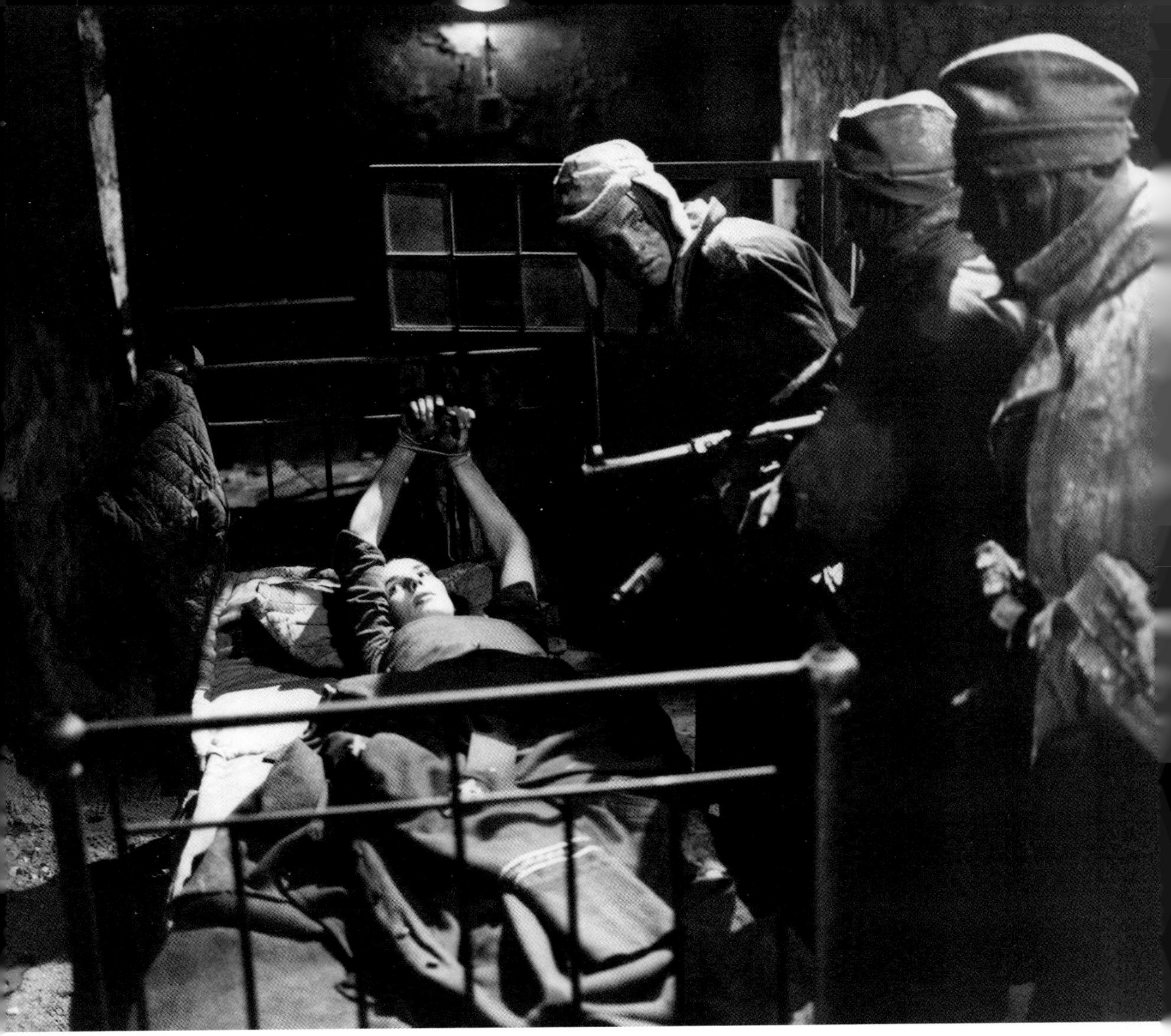

Seeking shelter in Haller's command post warehouse, they find it stocked to the full with supplies, clothing, food and wine. In a side room, they discover a Russian female prisoner, tied to a bed. It is Irina, the woman met by Hans in the sewers. The others retreat from the room ('It is done in order of rank', says one of them), but Hans cannot bring himself to rape her. (Bavaria Film)

With Hollywood films, such statements, if made at all, often serve only to try to assuage public disquiet over gratuitous violence on the screen, but such assurances from German film makers should be accepted more as genuine efforts to come to terms with the past and a real concern over political developments of the early 1990s. When asked why *Stalingrad* should be made now, Vilsmaier said: 'The experiences of Stalingrad have a disconcerting actuality. To name but a few examples: xenophobia coupled with German superiority; the rise of right-wing extremism, interested in falsifying German history; the growing tendency to solve problems in a militaristic way – see Yugoslavia, the Caucasus, etcetera, etcetera.'

Announced as 'the main film event of early 1993', *Stalingrad* had its world premiere at the Mathäser Filmpalast cinema in Munich on January

19, 1993. Even before the premiere, it was awarded the Bavarian Film Prize for best overall film production, with Vilsmaier receiving the prize for best conception and best camera, and sound chief Nikkei the award for best sound editing. Following a well-conducted publicity campaign, the film was released with 200 copies in cinemas throughout Germany. Over half a million Germans went to see the film in its first two weeks of showing.

As could be expected, reception of the film was decidedly mixed. Critics' reviews varied from mildly positive to outright negative. Gebhard Holzl of *Treffpunkt Kino* described it as 'a courageous, honest film', acceptable both

Irina speaks good German (she is an army interpreter) and they talk. In the other room, the atmosphere is unreal, almost dreamlike. While the battle rages outside, the men drink and play cards. They know they are doomed and each reacts to it in his own way. Hauptmann Musk, in his dying fever, gives incoherent orders for a final effort. His friend Otto, with a disillusioned, final 'Heil Hitler', kills himself with a bullet through the mouth. (Bavaria Film)

'Rollo' drags the dying Musk out of the building, only to witness General Hentz and his staff surrendering to the Russians. The 6. Armee has capitulated. With dead eyes, reduced to a fighting hulk, 'Rollo' refuses to take in that he is a prisoner. He prepares to seek the main battle line. In the house, Hans and Fritz prepare to give themselves up. Irina offers to guide them to the Russian lines but, as they wander across the snowy plain outside Stalingrad, the Russians open fire on them. Irina is killed and Hans wounded. All alone and completely lost, Fritz drags his wounded lieutenant across the windswept snow desert. Overcome by exhaustion, they sit down and slowly freeze to death. The icy wind covers the bodies with snow until they are no more than a white mound in a white landscape. The silence of death hangs over Stalingrad. (Bavaria Film)

from the artistic and ethical point of view. He judged Vilsmaier's direction of the film 'saddlefast', with special praise for the careful staging of the battle scenes and the accuracy of the art direction. Urs Jenny of *Der Spiegel* concluded that Vilsmaier had made 'gun-cracking war cinema, but with a bad conscience, never full out, never triumphant, always black-edged'. Though praising Vilsmaier's 'secure grip' on his actors and the whole project, Jenny criticised the screenplay, crying down the characters as too stereotypical and the end as too melodramatic. He thought the narration 'as heavy-going as the terrain . . . passing the usual stations of well-worn and typical dogface misery, never finding a unique, surprising, sweeping moment, an image that shows the monstrosity of it all'. He also found the film's deliberate lack of an image of the enemy, its avoidance to label the enemy as 'bad guys', unrealistic: 'not an evil word against the Russians leaves the lips of the main characters, not one evil Russian appears on the screen'.

Perhaps not surprisingly, the scene that evoked most discussion, both in the press and among viewers, was the one of the Russian prisoners being shot. Some people objected to it because it appears to spoil the image of the ordinary soldier as the main 'victim' of Stalingrad, and to again brand the Germans as a nation of war criminals. Others thought just the reverse, giving the opinion that it made the Germans look too good, since it shows the soldiers in the all too uncommon role of protesting against an obviously criminal order (although their protest seems not so much against the execution as such as prompted by the fact that their Russian 'friend' Kolja is among the people lined up). Almost every viewer in Germany linked the film's clear anti-war statement to the then current discussion about the desirability of possible future commitment of Bundeswehr forces in a United Nations context.

In the final analysis, Vilsmaier's idea to portray the mass suffering of the historic battle of 1942-43 and convey the senselessness and stupidity of war in general, through the experiences of a small group of men, does not seem to work out. Although well-played, the characters do not really come alive. For some reason, the process of identification, necessary for a film to get a grip on its audience, does not take place. As the drama unfolds, one remains an uninvolved bystander.

At the same time, Vilsmaier seems to have overlooked the fact that if one wants to tell the disintegration and destruction of a whole army through the experiences of one small platoon, one has at least to give plausible and sustained indications that this platoon is representative for thousands of others, all of them caught up in the same drama. The film has some notable mass scenes, but these are offset by several other scenes where the group is seen all by itself in a vast wasteland of snow with no other troops in sight (a notable example is the scene after the tank battle, when the group, reduced to half a dozen men, is seen man-handling an anti-tank gun across a windswept snowy plain). In short, despite the director's good intentions, the film somehow fails to do justice to the sheer magnitude of the tragedy of 50 years before.

In many ways, *Stalingrad* resembled the last major World War 2 feature film released before it, the 1990 Warner production *Memphis Belle*: a fictional story against the background of a true event; the excitement and horror of war encapsulated in the experiences of a small group of young men; the deliberate non-use of established box office stars; the attempt at authenticity and the attention for technical details and historical accuracy.

Looked at it thus, *Stalingrad* could be seen as the German compendium to that American movie, the two setting the trend for Second World War films that were to come out later.

Stalingrad was sold to most European countries and to Japan, and premiered in Canada and the United States in May 1995. It was released on DVD in 2006.